The Monologue Audition

The Monologue Audition

A Practical Guide for Actors

by Karen Kohlhaas

Limelight Editions

Published by Limelight Editions (an imprint of Amadeus Press, LLC)
512 Newark Pompton Turnpike
Pompton Plains, New Jersey 07444, USA

Website: www.limelighteditions.com

Printed in the United States of America

Reprinted in October 2005

Library of Congress Cataloging-in-Publication Data

Kohlhaas, Karen.
     The monologue audition : a practical guide for actors / by Karen Kohlhaas
        p. cm.
     ISBN 0-87910-291-8
        1. Acting—Auditions. 2. Monologues. I. Title.

     PN2071.A92 K64 2000
     792'.028—dc21

00-035717

CONTENTS

Part 2: Acting Your Monologue

Part 3: Auditioning with Your Monologue

Dedication

I am indebted to David Mamet, as I feel other members of the Atlantic Theater Company and all of our students have been over the years, for teaching us early in our theatrical lives about simple dramatic action, the truth of the moment, focusing on what is in our control and not bothering with what isn't, and about the value in this business of courtesy, self-esteem, hard work, and professionalism. I am indebted also to Anthony Di Pietro, from whom I took a wonderful directing class in 1993. He taught me as practical an approach to directing as Mamet had to acting, with which I learned how a director can serve the play by putting ideas concretely, beautifully, and consistently on the stage. This book is dedicated to them.

Acknowledgments

Many thanks to the friends who read the manuscript in several versions and generously gave their opinions, encouragement and suggestions: Diana Amsterdam, Emily Caigan, Rick Gradone and Paul Marcarelli. Many thanks also to the actors who have taken the workshop over the years for their enthusiasm, including those who agreed to be photographed for this book: Diana Ascher, Cynthia Carrol, Jen Davis, Yolanda Hester, Aurora Jones, Dan Laughlin, Scott Mackin, Paul Marcarelli, Juan Pareja, and George Roberson III. Very special thanks to Peter S. Cane, Esq.

Foreword

I've always enjoyed thinking about monologues.

Actors historically complain that the soliloquy form is unnatural, dated, and impossible—"How can I talk to someone when there's no one there?"

The soliloquy, in truth, is the most often-performed of dramas—we do it in the shower, on the bus, while walking, we address the boss who has wronged us, the love from whom we want a last chance, the parent from whom we want an explanation—we perform it before the event, full of resolve, and after the event, full of chagrin ("If I could do that over again, here's what I'd say...").

These monologues are not static but full of life. The absence of "the other" does not limit the performer in any way (you will note that the great speech of contrition, indictment, confession, explanation, can be performed not once, but many times, refining itself magically with each repetition—we've all done it on that solitary walk).

This book treats the monologue-soliloquy in its specialized appearance as The Audition.

In this incarnation the actor must not only choose an objective as above but devise a bit of *blocking* (thus acting, also, as a self-director), and, as if that weren't enough, take an overview of the whole process as a piece of self-promotion.

The audition process is an abomination. It is, generally, a tool for unsure and unimaginative casting agents, and directors. But, turn it on its head, and we have, as Ms. Kohlhaas suggests, an opportunity to investigate and improve one's understanding of script analysis, staging, and self-promotion. What a good idea.

David Mamet

Introduction

This book is for any actor who auditions with monologues. I began in theater as an actor, and I hated most of my monologue auditions! I didn't know how to act without a partner; I didn't know what to do with my body; and I didn't know where I should focus my attention. I had no idea how my auditions were coming across, or how to make them better. It wasn't until I became a director and a teacher that I was able to watch monologues from the other side. I saw many actors who seemed to feel the same way I had when I was auditioning.

A monologue audition seems to be an unfair request to make of an actor: he is asked to demonstrate what he is capable of doing in a few minutes, without any of the elements he would normally have to work with in a play. Very often a monologue audition makes an actor so uncomfortable that it's impossible for him to show those who audition him what kind of an actor he really is. Many actors I meet say that monologues were not addressed effectively during their training—even though a monologue is quite literally an actor's calling card when first entering the business.

It *is* unfair that the most commonly asked-for way of getting your work seen is for you to go into a room full of strangers and act all by yourself. The reality is that the request to do so from agents, directors, schools, and casting directors is not going to go away. If you, like many actors, dread monologue auditions and avoid them as much as possible, I suggest the only solution is to change your attitude toward them.

After watching many actors audition with monologues, I developed a workshop to address the problems and discomfort I saw over and over again. In it, I found that, if an actor embraces the challenges a monologue audition presents, and works on all of the elements of rehearsal, performance, and presentation in her control, she can make her monologue auditions into opportunities to show some very desirable (and hirable) qualities about herself as a performer—that she

- Puts time and care into her preparation
- Makes specific choices
- Acts those choices immediately and fully
- Uses her voice when she acts
- Has a professional attitude about her work
- Enjoys and takes pride in performing

An actor can also use monologue auditions to accumulate skills and experience that will benefit him in all of his performing. He can

- Grow by working on different kinds of material
- Get performing experience
- Expand the range of characters he can play
- Practice acting fully under pressure
- Develop a productive working relationship with himself

Finally, and most important, an actor can work on monologues to constantly feed her enthusiasm and determination about her choice to be an actor by

- Finding and working on the writing she loves the most
- Joining with other actors to work on monologues together in a supportive environment
- Challenging herself to learn and improve from every audition experience she has
- Using monologues as a way to work constantly and indulge her love of performing

This book is about bringing all of these qualities to your work on monologues and to your auditions. I hope it helps you create more enjoyment and success in your auditioning and performing life, and I hope your past frustrations with monologues will no longer stand in the way of you becoming the actor you want to be.

Preface: Working for Your Own Satisfaction

What is in your control about auditioning? What is not in your control about auditioning? Have you ever asked yourself these questions?

In the workshops I teach in New York, we start the first class by brainstorming answers to these two questions as a group. The following list has evolved out of those classes:

In My Control

Before the Audition
Knowing as much as possible
   about the audition
Planning effectively: material,
   clothes, how I will get there

Preparation
My choice of material
Paying attention to the length
   and style of monologues they
   request
Knowing the whole play
Making specific acting choices
How I stage the monologue
Having my lines memorized
Having my staging memorized
Rehearsing enough
Rehearsing with someone else
Rehearsing the whole audition

Not In My Control

Before the Audition
What the audition is for
The quality of the project
How much it pays
What they are looking for
When the audition is

Preparation

The Audition

Always being early
Being rested, and eating before the audition
Dressing appropriately and comfortably
Looking like my headshot/having one that looks like me
Having something productive to do while waiting
How I introduce myself
Where I put my attention while acting
Using my voice fully
Never starting over
Committing to my choices
Being willing to take direction
Listening carefully to how they direct me
Having other monologues ready
My attitude toward them
My attitude toward my performance
How I leave the room

The Audition

Delays getting there
How I feel
How many people they have to see
How many people are before me
How on schedule they are
The competition
What other actors say in the waiting room
Who's watching
The space
Their mood/tiredness
What kind of day they've had
Interruptions
How they perceive my "type"
Who I remind them of
Whether they cut me off
Whether they like my monologue
Whether they think it's "right" for me
What they say about my monologue
If and how they direct me
Quality of material they ask me to read
Who they ask me to read with
Their professionalism
Whether they know what they want
Whether they've already cast the part

After the Audition

How I talk to myself about how it went
Identifying what I learned from this audition
Taking steps to improve my next audition
Having something enjoyable to do afterward

After the Audition

When/if they get back to me
Whether I get a callback audition
Whether I get the part

Long Term

Finding out about and going on
    every audition I can

Having a repertoire of mono-
    logues that reflect my skills *and*
    the kind of work I want to do

Rehearsing regularly

Working on my voice, speech, and
    body

Staying in shape

Seeing movies and plays regularly

Reading plays constantly

Knowing who I want to work with

Setting my own standards for my
    work

My professionalism

Doing everything I can to make
    my work as enjoyable as
    possible

The attitude I take toward my
    work

Learning skills that will make me
    more employable (accents,
    improvisation, stage combat,
    on-camera)

Finding opportunities to be a
    reader for auditions so I can
    learn from the other side

Getting involved in the theaters
    around me

Making the most of every project
    I do

Producing my own projects for
    people to come see

Feeding my enthusiasm about
    acting

Having a positive and habitual
    approach to auditioning

How hard I work

**Working for my own
    satisfaction**

Long Term

Typecasting

How much work I get

How much work there is

The success of my peers

What any production I do leads to

Whether I "make it"

What age I will be if I do "make
    it"

How much longer I will have to
    do something else to pay my
    bills

I invite you to do the next step of this exercise here in this book:

- Mark the items on the "In My Control" side of the list that you regularly do.

- Mark the items on the "Not In My Control" side of the list that you regularly worry about or other wise put energy into.

Any surprises? I think anyone would agree that a life spent worrying about the "Not In My Control" side of the list will probably be miserable. I think noticing how many items there are on the "In My Control" side is pretty motivating and inspiring. You may also find it's actually liberating to recognize how much about this business isn't in your control at all.

We usually get most upset about things not in our control: "How dare they keep me waiting all afternoon!" "Why were they rude to me?" "Why didn't they call me back?" Yet, we tend to procrastinate when it comes to the things that are most likely to benefit us: "One of these days I'll get around to taking that voice class/getting new pictures/working on Shakespeare/ finding new monologues." Simply recognizing what is in your control about auditioning and what isn't is the first step toward redirecting your energy from unproductive worrying into habits and activities that will make your auditions more effective and you happier as an actor.

Notice that there is *nothing* about your preparation that is not in your control! Parts 1 and 2 of this book are about the unlimited control you have over the directing and acting of your monologues. This book also addresses many of the other items on the "In My Control" side. Following are several I think are important to talk about before we begin.

Working for Your Own Satisfaction

As you can see on the "Not In My Control" side, getting the part is *not* in your control. As you can also see, there are many reasons why you might not get a part that have nothing to do with your actual audition. Judging your success as an actor, especially early in your career, by whether or not you get a particular part can easily lead to frustration and despair. I suggest instead that you set a goal for your auditions that *is* in your control: *working for your own satisfaction.* Notice how long the "Long Term" section is on the "In My Control" side. A life in show business spent on that side of the list can be incredibly satisfying. Do you see that this kind of thinking can also make your auditions more successful?

Finding and Choosing Monologues

Finding material to work on is a huge stumbling block for many actors: "What is my type?" "Which monologues are 'overdone'?" "I can't audition because I can't find the 'right' material." Actors usually limit themselves this way because they only do monologues when absolutely necessary, and they feel uncertain about how to prepare them. This book is about solving those problems. In the meantime, this is my definition of a monologue that is "right" for you:

- It tells a complete story—it has a beginning, middle, climax, and end (the directing chapters will help you make this decision).

- It should be *conceivably* within your playing range (use your common sense—but break this rule when you want to, as described below).

- You should like the writing enough to work on it.

- It should be an appropriate length for most auditions—most commonly two minutes or shorter.

- It should not require complicated props.

Beyond these commonsense considerations, the field is open for your choices.

Many actors try to make one or two monologues into "workhorses," pieces they use for all their auditions. This practice works against the actor and the material. If you try to make one monologue do everything for you, your interpretation and playing of it will probably be generalized. Instead, I suggest you work to build a repertoire of specifically chosen monologues based on the kind of auditions you go on most and the kind of work you want to do. Instead of one or two, have ten! That's only twenty minutes of material. Have several contrasting monologues that cover the categories of classical/contemporary and comedy/drama. After that, use your selections to specialize, and to have fun. Do a monologue that demonstrates your mastery of a particular accent. Work on extreme kinds of writing and characters that may be good for specific auditions. If you love absurdism, farce, or film noir, work on those kinds of pieces. Work on writing that moves you, or that expresses your particular crazy sense of humor. The possibilities are endless.

I've heard many stories of the opinions given by agents and casting directors about the monologues actors perform for them: "That monologue isn't right for your type." "That monologue is perfect for you." "Don't do material that everyone knows." "Only do material that everyone knows." Why drive yourself crazy listening to this contradictory advice? I think the only solution is to have enough variety in your repertoire so that, in any of these situations, you could say "Okay, I also have one from _____."

I've heard of just as many experiences in which an actor has actually changed the kind of roles her agent sends her out on because she performed a monologue that was "against" what he thought was her "type," or in which an actor got a part because he took a risk in his choice of material.

Know the venue for each audition. Many casting directors and agents want to see you do monologues close to your age, ethnicity, and personality. Graduate schools usually want the classical/contemporary, comedy/drama combination. Experimental theater companies may *want* you to play a part completely away from your type!

As for sources beyond the monologue books, look at movies, novels, interviews with interesting people, collections of letters, short stories, poems, radio plays, books of comedic essays, and even television shows and newspaper articles. A friend of mine found a "monologue" in a documentary about David Lynch in which Lynch made a fascinating statement about his work. Make your search for material a way that you keep up with new writing, current events, history, or anything else that interests you and feeds your creativity.

You may find that the concept of "directing your monologue" presented in Part 1 makes you look at monologues differently. Once you realize how much you can influence a piece with your direction, you may see possibilities in material you wouldn't have seen before.

Recently in a monologue workshop I requested that each actor take a chance with his or her next choice of material for class. I asked that everyone purposely choose a monologue that in some way would be a huge personal challenge. One actor did a monologue that required she sing during parts of it; one performed in verse; one learned a Polish accent; one worked on an extremely vulnerable character; one played three different characters within one monologue, and so on. The results were thrilling because these actors chose their material for different reasons than most actors choose audition monologues. Because their choices were specific and personal—and required a lot of each actor in order to make the monologues work—those of us watching saw performers who were invested in challenging themselves. These performances were much more exciting to watch than "actors doing appropriate audition monologues well."

Taking control of your choice of material makes you active. Instead of passively listening to everyone else's opinions about what you should do, use your common sense, set your *own* goals, and challenge yourself—you will have a greater investment in your work.

Working on My Voice, Speech, and Body

I ask this in every acting class I teach: "Think of someone you know who is a working professional of some kind—but *not* an actor or performer—who has a beautiful, powerful, expressive voice. Is he good at what he does? Is he successful in his profession?" The response to these questions 99 percent of the time is *yes*. I have asked hundreds of people these questions and I think this is an astounding response. It means there *must* be a relationship between the quality of a person's voice, his willingness to become good at something, and his success. The next question is obvious: "If people who aren't performers succeed because of their voices, then how much *more* important is voice to an *actor?"*

David Mamet has said that voice work is the easiest, cheapest way to happiness as an actor. He has also said that most actors will never work on their voices enough. So many actors spend a fortune on pictures and acting classes but invest little in their voices, speech, and physical skills.

Improving your vocal and physical skills are concrete ways you can be ready for your breaks when they come. Failing to do so can lose you roles. Vocal and speech problems limit casting of every kind. Working on your voice means not only working on projection but on making your voice beautiful and expressive. Sure, you can get some work without working on your voice. But voice and speech are reasons why film and television actors often have difficulty handling substantial stage roles. Imagine you've been cast in the lead of a three-hour production that is going to have eight performances a week for a long run. Do you have the vocal stamina *now* that you will need to perform it?

Good speech can be a make-or-break skill in an audition. All the time and money you may spend on acting, movement, and even voice production classes is a waste if you simply cannot be understood. Muddy speech hurts your ability to get cast. An actor who can effortlessly articulate the most difficult language always stands head and shoulders above other actors of otherwise equal ability. Actors often have to unlearn patterns of speaking they grew up with that make them difficult to understand. Sure, "poor speech" may be needed for a particular character, but make that a choice rather than a limitation.

Working on your body means not only building your strength and stamina but your physical grace, fluidity, and expression. There are many ways of achieving these ends, including alignment training, dance, and martial arts. Each will improve your health and make acting more enjoyable as you learn to express yourself more fully with your whole body.

Finally, working to have an expressive voice, a graceful body, and clear speech means you have a desire to communicate and to be understood. The will to work on them is the will to go on stage and act the play. As David Mamet has also said, "Develop one of the most beautiful voices in the American theater, and you will *demand* the role." Actors with exquisite voices are so rare that directors can't afford to pass them up. Work on your voice, speech and body, and you will stand out from the actors who haven't bothered.

When you work on the material in this book, warm up your voice and body before every rehearsal and see how it makes your work more productive and enjoyable. Constantly ask your rehearsal partners whether they can hear and understand you easily. If you do so you will quickly learn the difference between how using your voice and body feels to you and how well it is actually coming across to your audience. If you have never worked on these skills, or if it has been a long time, find some good classes and see how much more fun and satisfaction you get out of acting.

Knowing Who I Want to Work With

Who are your favorite playwrights? Which directors would you kill to work with? Which actors inspire you? What are your ideal roles? If you are just entering the acting business, you may feel like you'll take any part you can get. However, I assume you chose to be an actor because you want to do certain kinds of work. Defining your ideal working experiences makes you form your own definitions of satisfaction as an actor. It reminds you what you are doing all of this work *for.*

An actor who thinks he will be happy just to be cast in *something* is sabotaging himself. Suppose he does get cast, but in a mediocre project with an inexperienced director. When the experience proves to be frustrating, it will be easy for him to believe he doesn't enjoy acting after all. On the other hand, an actor who has a very clear idea of the kinds of situations she wants to work in has an advantage. She may take a nonideal role for a specific reason (to get her work seen, to make contacts, to get experience); but she will know what she is getting into because she has a standard. She won't expect it to be a perfect experience, and she will be more likely to make the most of it.

To define your ideal work experiences, see movies and plays as often as possible. Read constantly. Keep a list of playwrights, directors, actors, filmmakers, and theater companies on every professional level whose work most appeals to you. Expand your horizons by seeing types of work you've never seen before.

How to Use This Book

I hope you will use this book not only to rehearse for an audition or two but to make working on monologues a fun, creative part of your acting life. If you think about it, you have more control over your monologue auditions than over any other part of your performing. How often does an actor get to choose, direct, *and* perform the material in a production?

In my workshops and in writing this book, I have tried to isolate and address every quality an actor would want to have present in a monologue audition. These qualities are broken down into categories and steps so that you can specifically identify them and work on them. Starting with one monologue, give yourself enough time, on a relaxed and regular schedule, to learn and practice each step until you have brought your monologue to performance level. After you have done this you can use the material as you need to for any other monologues you may choose.

Directing and Acting

In this book I separate the directing of your monologue from the acting of your monologue. An ideal director-actor relationship is one in which both parties make choices that are tried, modified, and rehearsed into the final production. The actor experiments from "inside" the play; the director makes suggestions from her perspective "outside." When you are rehearsing a monologue, you are the actor *and* the director, and the goal of this book is to give you that ideal working relationship *with yourself.*

I define *directing* your monologue as everything you *always* want to do physically when you perform it. You may never have thought about directing yourself in a monologue before. In my experience, too many actors prepare their audition monologues only "from the inside." They make interpretive choices for them-

selves as actors, but they often don't consider what the monologue looks like to those watching. Don't worry if you think,
"But I'm not a director!" Anyone who is moved or amused by a
story can learn to express those qualities with clear, physical,
repeatable staging. You may choose to have a lot of staging or a
little, depending on the piece. What's important is your being
aware of all the options you do have.

In "Part 1: Directing The Monologue," you'll learn to look at
a monologue "from the outside"—like a director would. You'll
develop a vocabulary of choices you can apply to stage your
monologue specifically and suspensefully. After you've completed and rehearsed your staging, you'll be free to commit to
your acting. Often actors find that learning how to direct their
monologues solves most of the problems they've been having
in auditions because having specific staging makes them less
nervous. Their palms may be sweating, but their bodies know
what to *do* when they get in there.

I define *acting* your monologue as *how* you perform your
staging *in the moment* to pursue the acting choices you've made
for your monologue. In "Part 2: Acting Your Monologue," you'll
learn how to make these choices, and how to play them fully.

The acting work for monologues in this book is based on
Practical Aesthetics, the acting technique we teach at the Atlantic Theater Company Acting School. Practical Aesthetics was
developed by David Mamet, who along with William H. Macy
taught it to us in the mid-1980's while we were drama students
at New York University. Many of us went on to found the Atlantic, and several members of the original classes coauthored
A Practical Handbook for the Actor (1986) which gives a more
complete description of the philosophies behind the technique.

I have found Practical Aesthetics to be an ideal technique for
rehearsing monologues. It helps you choose one simple acting
objective, called an *Action,* to play and ways to act the moments of your monologue truthfully, spontaneously, and powerfully. Most important for auditioning, you can use this technique to act your monologues just as truthfully *without having
to focus on a partner!* This factor is very important because
most auditors don't want you to address your monologue to
them when you audition.

The first time through this material, it's important to focus on
the work at hand by keeping the acting and directing absolutely

separate: When you're directing, maintain the director's perspective of "how I want it to look," and "kick the actor out of the room!" Free yourself to make bold choices for your staging. When you are working on the acting, "kick the director out of the room!" Don't worry about what it looks like, and let yourself take risks and experiment with acting the moments of your monologue.

In chapter 7, you'll put the acting back together with the directing of your monologue. The result will be like a well-directed and well-acted play: your monologue will have a clear structure that tells your story every time, *and* it will have committed, truthful acting in the moment.

The directing and acting chapters are grouped together so that you can see where each is going from start to finish. When I teach this material in a workshop, the actors alternate their work between the two, with assignments in each to do every week. I suggest reading through both parts 1 and 2 to get an idea of the scope of the material. Then do a step or two of each at a time, alternating your work on the directing and the acting, remembering to keep them separate.

If you give yourself enough time to explore and really learn both the acting and the directing material with your first monologue, you will find that your next monologues can come together very quickly. The acting and directing perspectives will have become part of you, and you'll know how to use each one the most effectively for the needs of the particular monologue you're working on.

Auditioning

In "Part 3: Auditioning with Your Monologue," I address all the "nonacting" part of an audition. How you handle the moments before and after you perform a monologue is very important because it is then that your auditors get a sense of how professional you are and what you could be like to work with. I specifically discuss what you can communicate about yourself in these nonacting moments, and how to make them into ways of presenting yourself confidently and professionally. In chapter 9 I present a way to talk to yourself productively after you audition, which if done faithfully will help you benefit from every audition you go on. In chapter 9 I also suggest several audition exercises to practice with other actors. These exercises test your focus and concentration, and give you ways of dealing with any audition environment you may encounter.

Work with Other Actors

To learn this material most completely and effectively, it is essential that you work with one or more partners. Some of the directing work can be done on your own, but the acting exercises always require another person to be in the room with you (in a pinch, you can ask someone to do this who is not an actor working on this material). Actors do not rehearse to perform by themselves in a room, with no audience! Having someone there gives you the needed pressure and focus you need for auditioning and performing. I think it's impossible truly to act a monologue alone. How many times have you tried to rehearse by yourself, stopping and starting, not knowing if something worked or not, or what you actually just did?

Ideally you will work with a small group of other actors who are as committed as you are to improving at monologue auditions. As you build good working relationships, you can give each other feedback and learn from watching each other. Something you get stuck on may come more easily to someone else and vice versa. And it's wonderful to be part of a motivated group, all dedicated to growing as performers.

Choosing Your First Monologue

Use the guidelines in the preface to choose a two-minute monologue with contemporary language in which your character is talking to one other character. The techniques in this book work in exactly the same way for classical monologues, although it is important that you also take the time to understand and speak the language clearly, which is why I suggest starting with a contemporary piece. Soliloquies (in which the character is alone on stage) and monologues in which the character is addressing multiple other characters are addressed later in the book.

PART 1
Directing Your Monologue

CHAPTER 1

STORY, SUSPENSE, AND STRUCTURE

Although you can apply the work in this book to monologues from any source, most audition monologues are taken from plays. When you audition with a monologue from a play, you are performing the piece in a circumstance different from the one the playwright originally intended. You don't have the rest of the play to give the monologue its context. You absolutely must know the script for what it will tell you about the importance of the monologue, but the monologue must stand on its own. Your choices immediately become stronger and more focused if you think of your monologue as one *Story*.

Telling the Story

The first step in directing your monologue is to examine it closely within the whole play, so that you understand what the story of this particular monologue means to the character. This understanding will make you form some opinions about how you think the author intended the monologue to be performed.

Here is a monologue from *Summer and Smoke* by Tennessee Williams. As you read about the choices I've made for this piece, apply the same steps to the monologue you have chosen to work on.

ALMA

You needn't try to comfort me. I haven't come here on any but equal terms. You said, let's talk truthfully. Well, let's do! Unsparingly, truthfully, even shamelessly, then! It's no longer a secret that I love you. It never was. I loved you as long ago as the time I asked you to read the stone angel's name with your fingers. Yes, I remember the long afternoons of our childhood, when I had to stay indoors to practice my music—and heard your playmates calling you, "Johnny, Johnny!" How it went through me, just to hear your name called! And how I—rushed to the window to watch you jump the porch railing! I stood at a distance, halfway down the block, only to keep in sight of your torn red sweater, racing about the vacant lot you played in. Yes, it had begun that early, this affliction of love, and has never let go of me since, but kept on growing. I've lived next door to you all the days of my life, a weak and divided person who stood in adoring awe of your singleness, of your strength. And that is my story! Now I wish you would tell me—why didn't it happen between us? Why did I fail? Why did you come almost close enough—and no closer?

Following are some questions to ask yourself about your monologue. While you absolutely can't "act the whole play" in the performance of a particular monologue, considering the questions gives you a place to start in your direction. If your monologue is not from a play or from a complete story, answer as many of them as you can. Doing so will give you the information you need to start the direction of any monologue.

Introductory Questions

- Who is the character addressing?

- Where does this monologue appear in the play?

- What has happened up to this point in the play (including the scene the monologue is in)?

- Why is this character speaking this monologue now?

- What does the character want the other character(s) to do as a result of hearing this monologue?

- What are the stakes? (What will happen if my character doesn't get what she wants?)

- Does the character succeed or fail?

Now use your responses to guide you in deciding how you envision the monologue ideally being performed. Answer this question:

- What is the *Story*? (How would I describe my vision of this monologue?)

Here are my answers to these questions for Alma's monologue:

- *Who is the character addressing?* John, with whom she has been in love her entire life.

- *Where does this monologue appear in the play?* In the last scene between Alma and John, the second to last scene in the play.

- *What has happened up to this point in the play?* John has returned to town after medical school. Alma, the preacher's daughter, saw his return as their opportunity to be together at last. Her upright sensibilities clashed with his wilder nature. John attempted to sleep with Alma, and she refused. His father was killed in a brawl, and John has now vowed to reform his ways and take over his father's medical practice. Alma has just found out that John is now engaged to Nellie, Alma's former music student. Alma still wants him so much that she has decided to change over to "his ways" and has come to make a final attempt at winning him.

- *Why is this character speaking this monologue now?* Alma has found out that John and Nellie are engaged. It is her last chance to reach him.

- *What does the character want the other character(s) to do as a result of hearing this monologue?* She wants John to decide to be with her instead of Nellie.

- *What are the stakes? (What will happen if my character doesn't get what she wants?)* Alma will lose the love of her life to someone else.

- *Does the character succeed or fail?* I think she fails.

- *What is the Story?* Alma makes a courageous, last-ditch attempt to win John by boldly addressing him as an equal and confessing her love for him. After describing the pain and excitement of being in love with him her whole childhood, she insistently demands to know why they never came together. Realizing she has failed, she ends the monologue crushed, still begging him to answer her.

Making decisions about the Story you want to tell with your monologue is the first in a series of steps that results in the staging of your monologue. I want to emphasize that the above example is *my* interpretation of this particular monologue. Someone else might end up with a different version of the Story. One might decide that Williams's intention was for Alma to end the monologue hopefully, expecting that John will want to be with her after she's bared her soul to him.

When you read any story or play or novel, your mind automatically provides an interpretation that is the most compelling one to y*ou* of what the author wrote. When you write out the Story of your monologue, it should describe what you want the audience to see when it is performed the way you see it in your mind's eye.

Your opinions of the Story are all you have to interpret the writer's intentions. Alana Valentine, an Australian playwright I worked with, said, "Everyone talks about serving the *playwright,* as if the playwright was the biggest authority on the play, or the 'boss' of the play. What they don't realize is that the playwright along with everybody else is there to serve the *play*." To hear a playwright say this was very liberating to me as a director because I had thought I must always serve the writer, or what theater scholars and critics insisted the writer meant. Thinking of myself as serving the play with my own opinions gave me permission to try them and change them as my understanding of the play developed.

If you find that deciding and writing out the Story for your monologue is hard to do, just make some working choices for now. You are free to change them, and probably will, as you work on the monologue.

Suspense

All of the directing choices I discuss from here on involve the element of *suspense.* I'm talking not about horror-movie suspense but about a deliberate, well-chosen flow of action that is specific to each part of the story. I think good direction is always suspenseful.

Suspenseful direction never lets the audience get ahead of the story, especially in a two-minute monologue. It lets the audience know from the start that they are in good hands. We've all had the experience as audience members of being in the hands of a confused director. When the direction of a movie or play is unclear or repetitive, the audience members get ahead of the story and try to predict what will happen next. If they don't like what they predict, they get restless and bored (you know this is happening when audience members start coughing or shifting around in their seats).

When you use suspense to direct your monologue, your specific, one-time choices quickly make your audience realize they don't quite know what's going to happen next, and they will have to pay attention in order to find out. I consider suspense below as I discuss the structural choices for your monologue, and throughout the process of staging your monologue.

Structure: Beginning, Middle, Climax, and End

Ever since we were little and stories were told to us, and all through our growing up seeing movies, television shows, and plays, we've had one dramatic structure imprinted upon us: *beginning, middle, climax,* and *end.* When we see a poorly structured production—a play with an incomplete ending, for example—we are left with a sense of dissatisfaction, of not really knowing what the writer was trying to say. We've been irritated by movies in which the story climaxed and yet the movie continued on and on as if the writer and director didn't know where to stop. Sometimes movies and plays lose us in the middle because of unclear or repetitive action—dialogue and scenes that don't tell us anything new. Sometimes they bore us in the very beginning with too much exposition and not enough action.

Any of these problems can come from the writing, the direction, or both. They're interdependent. Unclear direction can make a good script boring and repetitive, and a vague script can often be at least partially salvaged with specific direction. Obviously, for your monologue you want both: good writing, which is why your choice of material is important, and good direction to make clear, committed choices for the Story.

Monologues don't always have clear structure in the writing. Maybe a monologue you work on will be pieced together from several of one character's lines. Maybe you'll choose a monologue that is not from a play at all. And all monologues you audition with that are from plays will be performed out of context. In all cases, it's important to make clear choices about the beginning, middle, and end, and also about the climax. Having this clarity in structure gives your audience a sense of being told a complete Story. (If, after reading the rest of this section, you find it impossible to make these choices for a particular monologue, it may be a clue that it is not a good monologue to work on.)

Often the choices of beginning, middle, climax, and end are clearly present in the writing, but just as often there is quite a bit of room for interpretation. To decide the most effective beginning, middle, and end sections for your monologue, look for a sense of suspense—of "What's going to happen next?"—in the writing. Identifying these "cliffhangers" and using them to mark the sections immediately creates suspense in your direction. I use the example of Alma's monologue for this book because it has several possible suspenseful choices for each section.

The Beginning

Let's look at some choices for the beginning of Alma's monologue:

> ALMA
>
> You needn't try to comfort me. I haven't come here on any but equal terms.

This choice is suspenseful because the words tell us she is ready for a confrontation of some kind. Another choice:

> ALMA
>
> You needn't try to comfort me. I haven't come here on any but equal terms. You said, let's talk truthfully. Well, let's do! Unsparingly, truthfully, even shamelessly, then! It's no longer a secret that I love you. It never was.

This choice for the beginning tells us Alma has come to tell Johnny something important, and it tells us what that something is: she has loved him for a long time. We hear her confession and wonder what is going to happen next. Another choice:

ALMA

You needn't try to comfort me. I haven't come here on any but equal terms. You said, let's talk truthfully. Well, let's do! Unsparingly, truthfully, even shamelessly, then!

In my opinion, this is the most suspenseful choice for the beginning. For Alma (the preacher's daughter) to say she's going to talk "shamelessly" is a big deal. It gives me even more of a sense of "What's going to happen next?".

Because audition monologues are only a couple of minutes long, most are best served by putting the beginning in the earliest place possible, the first moment you feel your audience would be in suspense. Therefore, it's fine to choose a very short beginning:

ROMEO

But soft! What light through yonder window breaks?
Romeo and Juliet by William Shakespeare

TREVES

The most striking feature about him was his enormous head.
The Elephant Man by Bernard Pomerance

These short beginnings have done their job, which is to set up the suspense and leave us wondering what is going to happen next. However, I've also seen many longer beginnings in which the story has been set up a bit more by the writer before the suspense is clear:

MAX

Either you do or you don't. That's all! It's as simple as that. No! I'm not listening to any more arguments. If you love me like you say you do, you put on that lingerie for me.
Lingerie by Diana Amsterdam

JOAN

Yes: they told me you were fools, and that I was not to listen to your fine words nor trust to your charity. You promised me my life; but you lied. You think that life is nothing but not being stone dead. It is not the bread and water I fear:

> From *Saint Joan* by George Bernard Shaw

The Middle

Choosing the beginning and end of your monologue automatically defines the middle. There are no hard and fast rules for the lengths of the beginning, middle, and end, although the middle is almost always the longest section.

The End

Here are some possible ends for Alma's monologue. Which of the following, for you, is most suspenseful?

> I've lived next door to you all the days of my life, a weak and divided person who stood in adoring awe of your singleness, of your strength. And that is my story! **[End:]** Now I wish *you* would tell *me*—why didn't it happen between us? Why did I fail? Why did you come almost close enough—and no closer?

or

> I've lived next door to you all the days of my life, a weak and divided person who stood in adoring awe of your singleness, of your strength. And that is my story! Now I wish *you* would tell *me*—**[End:]** why didn't it happen between us? Why did I fail? Why did you come almost close enough—and no closer?

or

> I've lived next door to you all the days of my life, a weak and divided person who stood in adoring awe of your singleness, of your strength. And that is my story! Now I wish you would tell me—why didn't it happen between us? Why did I fail? **[End:]** Why did you come almost close enough—and no closer?

or

> I've lived next door to you all the days of my life, a weak and divided person who stood in adoring awe of your singleness, of your strength. And that is my story! Now I wish *you* would tell *me*—why didn't it happen between us? Why did I fail? Why did you come almost close

enough—**[End:]** and no closer?

Although I think each choice is suspenseful, I prefer the second, in which the end comes right after "Now I wish *you* would tell *me*—." After hearing Alma describe what a painful, life-long torture loving John has been for her, I am in the most suspense here, as she prepares to ask him for a response. The punctuation Williams uses here also supports this interpretation. Compared to the other choices, I would be the most on the edge of my seat as an audience member, wondering what she's going to say.

Ends can also be just one sentence, or even one word, depending on the monologue (notice in the fourth example that the end is just the final phrase of the piece). Keep in mind that, when the end is too long, we lose a sense of it truly being the end of the Story and risk losing the audience's attention. The end also has an important relationship to the climax. Read about choosing a climax below, and see if doing so influences where you want to put the end in your monologue.

The Climax

The *climax* is the moment of highest tension in the monologue. After the Story of your monologue climaxes, your audience expects the end to come soon. For this reason, the climax usually comes toward the end of the middle section or in the actual end section of the monologue. Very often the climax ends the middle, leaving the end to be the resolution.

The moment of highest tension means there can only be one climax in your monologue. Choosing a climax doesn't mean the other parts of the monologue are unimportant. It means instead that each other part has a specific meaning *in relation* to the climax and is therefore stronger and more defined. Making a specific choice of climax encourages you to make specific choices for all of the other parts, which makes your direction suspenseful and keeps your audience with you. It also shows your auditors that you know how to commit to a specific interpretation. When you choose your climax, keep in mind that it should be fairly short. When a climax lasts too long, it tends to lose its importance. At first, I thought I wanted the climax of Alma's monologue to be at the very end:

> **[End:]** why didn't it happen between us? Why did I fail?
> **[Climax:] Why did you come almost close enough—
> and no closer?**

I would make this choice for the climax if I felt that Alma only
builds in intensity during this monologue and doesn't give up.
After working on the monologue, however, I chose a different
climax:

> **[End and Climax:] why didn't it happen between
> us? Why did I fail?** Why did you come almost close
> enough—and no closer?

At first, I really thought the climax should be at the very end.
But as I discuss in chapter 4, after working on this monologue
I developed a strong opinion that, by the end, Alma knows she
has lost. As the scene between Alma and John goes on, he does
try to explain to her, but it doesn't matter (in my opinion). I
think she knows by the end of this monologue she won't ever
get what she really wants, which is for John to love her. The
second choice of climax supports this interpretation because
the line after it will, by definition, have less intensity than the
climax. (A note: The actor playing Alma, however, *will not*
give up. This point is made clear in the chapters on acting your
monologue.)

The reason I say "I think," and "in my opinion" is that there
is never a right way to direct or act anything. There is only your
way. Any monologue will affect you differently than it will anyone else. Your direction will be stronger if you express those
differences fully rather than minimize them. I am not encourag-
ing you to randomly do whatever strikes you but to study the
script carefully and listen to your own instincts about what the
writer is saying. Expressing your opinions fully in your direction tells your audience, "This is what this writer says to *me*
with this monologue," which is always more compelling than
"This is how 60 percent of scholars and 35 percent of theater
critics and my high school acting teacher say this monologue
should be performed."

When actors in my class first look for beginnings, middles,
ends, and climaxes in their monologues they are often surprised
and pleased to find that choosing the sections only takes a few
minutes. They're often also relieved to discover they *do* have

directing instincts, they *do* have some control over their interpretation, and all of a sudden the monologue seems a lot less daunting to them as a director *and* an actor.

I hope you are excited about starting the direction of your monologue, especially if you've never directed anything before. What are your first instincts about the most suspenseful choices for the beginning, middle, climax, and end? What options has the writer given you? How would each choice affect the interpretation? If you are torn between different choices, read your monologue aloud to yourself or someone else, pausing after each section. Experiment with different places for the climax. How might each choice of climax change the impact of the monologue? Which one do you think tells your Story best?

Checklist for Story, Suspense, and Structure

❏ You have answered the introductory questions and have written out the Story of your monologue.

❏ You have made the most suspenseful choices you could find for the beginning, middle, and end of your monologue.

❏ You have chosen the climax of your monologue.

CHAPTER 2

MAKING CHOICES

The first step toward creating suspenseful staging for your monologue was choosing the beginning, middle, climax, and end in chapter 1. The next is to get even more specific.

Chunks

A *Chunk* is a group of words or sentences within the beginning, middle, and end sections of your monologue that feels to you like a complete unit, like a single thought or point being made in the writing.

Dividing your monologue into Chunks lets you control how the audience receives the flow of information in the monologue, according to your interpretation. For example, you can create a short Chunk to draw attention to a sentence or phrase you want to highlight. You can create a longer Chunk if you feel the writer was making only one overall point in that section of the monologue. If you have a very short beginning or end, you can express that choice by defining it as one Chunk. Your middle section almost always contains several Chunks, and you can make the climax its own Chunk so that it stands out.

Creating Chunks for Your Monologue

Notice the following in the example from Alma's monologue:

- *No Chunk overlaps the divisions between beginning and middle and end.* It's fine, however, to start a new Chunk in the middle of a sentence of text, as I did after "Now I wish *you* would tell *me*—"

Section	Chunk
Beginning	You needn't try to comfort me. I haven't come here on any but equal terms
	You said, let's talk truthfully. Well, let's do! Unsparingly, truthfully, even shamelessly, then!
Middle	It's no longer a secret that I love you. It never was. I loved you as long ago as the time I asked you to read the stone angel's name with your fingers.
	Yes, I remember the long afternoons of our childhood, when I had to stay indoors to practice my music—and heard your playmates calling you, "Johnny, Johnny!" How it went through me, just to hear your name called!
	And how I—rushed to the window to watch you jump the porch railing! I stood at a distance, halfway down the block, only to keep in sight of your torn red sweater, racing about the vacant lot you played in.
	Yes, it had begun that early, this afflicion of love, and has never let go of me since, but kept on growing. I've lived next door to you all the days of my life, a weak and divided person who stood in adoring awe of your singleness, of your strength.
	And that is my story! Now I wish *you* would tell *me*—
End	**[Climax:] why didn't it happen between us? Why did I fail?**
	Why did you come almost close enough—and no closer?

- *The climax is its own Chunk.*

- *I made sure I did not choose too many or too few Chunks for this monologue.* If I had created too many Chunks—for example, a Chunk for each sentence—there would have been too many details. If I had created too few, the flow of the story would not be specific enough. For a two-minute monologue you should have between seven and ten Chunks.

- *The Chunks are of different lengths.* The Chunks in the middle of Alma's monologue are longer because I think each expresses one main thought. I used short Chunks to isolate what I felt were very important statements in the beginning and end of the monologue. In your monologue, you could even make one word a Chunk of its own, if you feel doing so is right for your piece.

- *The Chunks can follow shifts of mood and rhythm in the writing.* Notice that the first few sentences have a fast, sharp rhythm to them. When Alma starts talking to Johnny about her lifelong feelings for him, the sentences get longer and more fluid. When she ends her story and finally confronts him, her rhythm quickens and the sentences are shorter. Notice how the Chunks follow these changes.

- *The Chunks can change later on.* You're not locked into the Chunks you create now. When you stage your monologue, you'll have stronger opinions about how each Chunk contributes to the Story. If you need more specificity, you can separate one Chunk into two. If you think there are too many small Chunks, you can combine two of them into one longer one.

Look at your monologue and make quick, instinctive choices about dividing it into Chunks. Then, make sure your beginning, middle, climax, and end are still intact. Count the Chunks. Are there too many—more than ten? Too few—fewer than seven? Read it aloud, or ask someone to read it to you, pausing briefly after each Chunk. If you are torn between two choices, read it both ways, listening carefully for how each option tells the Story a little differently. Choose the one you like best.

Descriptions

Descriptions are staging tools that help you name the physical "picture" you want the audience to see in each Chunk as the monologue is performed.

It is very important that you understand what Descriptions are *not*. Descriptions are *only* a director's tool; they are *not* acting choices for your monologue. If you tried to act the Descriptions, your performance would seem preplanned and untruthful. As you will read in the chapters on acting your monologue, I want you to be free to let the moments of your monologue mean anything they need to mean when you act it, so that your performances are always fresh and spontaneous. Descriptions are simply a way to articulate your ideas from a director's *visual* perspective. Know that, once you've finished your Descrip-

Beginning	You needn't try to comfort me. I haven't come here on any but equal terms.	Nervously scolds
	You said, let's talk truthfully. Well, let's do! Unsparingly, truthfully, even shamelessly, then!	Resolutely challenges
Middle	It's no longer a secret that I love you. It never was. I loved you as long ago as the time I asked you to read the stone angel's name with your fingers.	Bravely confesses
	Yes, I remember the long afternoons of our childhood, when I had to stay indoors to practice my music—and heard your playmates calling you, "Johnny, Johnny!" How it went through me, just to hear your name called!	Bitterly complains
	And how I—rushed to the window to watch you jump the porch railing! I stood at a distance, halfway down the block, only to keep in sight of your torn red sweater, racing about the vacant lot you played in.	Excitedly confides
	Yes, it had begun that early, this afflicion of love, and has never let go of me since, but kept on growing. I've lived next door to you all the days of my life, a weak and divided person who stood in adoring awe of your singleness, of your strength.	Frustratedly lectures
	And that is my story! Now I wish *you* would tell *me*—	Abruptly regroups
End	**[Climax:] why didn't it happen between us? Why did I fail?**	Agitatedly demands
	Why did you come almost close enough—and no closer?	Brokenly begs

tions, you will turn them into staging—physical movements—and forget about their wording.

Descriptions use vivid, "seeable" adverbs and verbs to give each Chunk of your monologue its own identity. As you can see in my choices for Alma's monologue, each Description has an adverb and verb that together create the images I want the audience to see in each Chunk. Working with Descriptions is the next-best thing to having a director for every monologue you do because it helps you keep an outside-the-scene perspective as you decide what you want *your* audience to see.

Writing Descriptions helps you tell the Story clearly by defining how each Chunk uniquely relates to the climax. This practice will build the suspense by ensuring that your staging won't be vague or repetitive. To create Descriptions, choose a verb that describes *what* you imagine the character doing in that part of the Story and an adverb that describes *how* you imagine him doing it. As you can see in the following example, changing your choices of adverb and verb radically affects how the Chunk looks in the staging:

JOAN

But without these things I cannot live; and by your wanting to take them away from me, or from any human creature, I know that your counsel is of the devil, and that mine is of God.

Saint Joan by George Bernard Shaw

Imagine how different each of the following Descriptions would make this Chunk of Joan's monologue look:

- Furiously condemns
- Patiently teaches
- Casually dismisses

Descriptions are a condensed version of a technique I learned in directing class. Writing down what I wanted to see on stage was the most powerful directing tool anyone had ever taught me. It gave me a reliable way to record my choices for a scene as it evolved in rehearsal, and a way to test whether those choices were coming across clearly in the staging. If they weren't, I could restage the scene or change my description of it. Your Descriptions will often change as you get to know your monologue better as a director. Keeping track of your Descriptions provides a record of what the monologue currently looks like to you.

Again, when you're writing your Descriptions it's important to separate the actor from the director. Give the director in you complete freedom to make bold, vivid, passionate choices of Descriptions for each Chunk in your monologue. If the actor in you tries to get involved, or is afraid of the choices, kick him out of the room. Remind him that he is not responsible for acting the Descriptions—ever!

Choosing Descriptions for Your Chunks

If you look at the Story I created for Alma's monologue in chapter 1, you'll notice that several of the words I use there became ideas for my Descriptions. Here are some more guidelines for choosing Descriptions for your monologue:

- *The words of your Descriptions must be "seeable."* They must suggest immediate, vivid, physical pictures so you can turn them into specific staging. Therefore, it's fine if they seem melodramatic. (Remember, you won't be acting them.) To test whether your words are seeable, imagine each Description being performed silently. Can you clearly understand what the character is doing? Verbs like "asks" and "tells" are too vague because each can look many different ways. "Asks" can look like "demands," "begs," or "coaxes." "Tells" could look like "announces," "confesses," or "confides." The character may be "questioning," but that is too general. What kind of questioning? Interrogating? Begging? The adverbs, too, should be easy to see. Below are lists of some vague, "unseeable" verbs to avoid, and "seeable" verbs and adverbs to get you started. There are thousands more. You might find a thesaurus helpful in finding words for your Descriptions.

Unseeable, vague verbs *not* to use

Tells	Remembers	Questions
States	Recalls	Asks
Says	Reminisces	Answers
Informs	Describes	Discusses

Seeable verbs to use

Challenges	Condemns	Berates
Confronts	Savors	Jokes
Begs	Warns	Goads
Dismisses	Lectures	Coaxes
Announces	Ponders	Teaches
Dares	Regroups	Entreats
Flirts	Frets	Pleads
Gossips	Assures	Confesses

Teases	Vows	Invites
Taunts	Attacks	Complains
Mocks	Encourages	Apologizes
Revels	Grills	Threatens
Confides	Scolds	Orders

Seeable adverbs to use

Boldly	Mischievously	Coolly
Hesitantly	Arrogantely	Haughtily
Sincerely	Confidently	Apologetically
Happily	Eagerly	Viciously
Scornfully	Nervously	Lovingly
Sarcastically	Dreamily	Disgustedly
Hopelessly	Carefully	Exasperatedly
Shamefully	Hopefully	Giddily
Exhaustedly	Righteously	Casually
Frustratedly	Furiously	Shyly

- *Descriptions contain no plot.* Verbs like "remembers" and "reminisces" are from the plot. If we see "remembers" performed silently, we cannot tell what the character is doing. We can only see what the memory is doing to the character's behavior. Alma is remembering many different things in her monologue. I wanted the audience to see how each memory affects her, which led me to Descriptions like "bravely confesses," "excitedly confides," and "bitterly complains" for those Chunks.

- *A Descriptive adverb or verb should be used only once in the monologue.* The purpose of Descriptions is to make the staging of each Chunk unique to build the suspense. If the same adverbs and verbs are repeated, they lose their power to make each Chunk of the monologue specific.

- *Your adverb and verb should make a complete picture that makes sense.* Sometimes they can cancel each other out: for example, "angrily flirts" is impossible to see—we would see one word or the other.

- *Use your Descriptions to direct variety into your monologue.* Variety is very important. Many monologues run the risk of being "one note" because they're so short. One of the reasons I chose "excitedly confides" for Alma's monologue was to make sure it has variety. If your monologue seems to be "all angry" or "all desperate" or "all silly" in the overall tone of the writing, ask yourself which Chunk or Chunks can be different—more vulnerable, more confident, or more sincere. This variety gives your piece more depth and keeps it from becoming predictable, or "one note".

- *The Descriptions add up to a complete Story.* Compare your Descriptions to the Story you wrote for your monologue. Do your Descriptions tell your Story? Do you get a sense of suspense in the beginning, middle, and end? Is the Description for the climax vivid and expressive? It's also fine if working on the Descriptions inspires you to change parts of your Story.

- *Have fun with your Descriptions!* As you become familiar with using them, your choices of Descriptions can help express your sense of humor or drama about a particular Chunk. Allow yourself to experiment; don't worry about "getting it right"—there are no right answers.

Follow these guidelines to create a Description for each Chunk of your monologue. Remember, the test is, could you understand the Description if you saw it performed silently?

I find it effective to jot down my first impulses for all of the Descriptions, even if some Descriptions are incomplete or have duplicate words. Then, after a break I go back to it and get more specific. If I do have duplicate words, I ask myself how they are different from each other—if I have "threatens" twice, maybe I'll change one to "warns" instead.

If your Descriptions are absolutely seeable and follow the other guidelines, you are ready to go on. You can always adjust your Descriptions, and probably will when you start staging them and get more ideas.

Sizes and Speeds

Sizes and Speeds are another incredibly powerful directing tool and are the next step toward your staging. There are only four: *Big and Fast, Small and Fast, Small and Slow, Big and Slow.* To experience how Sizes and Speeds look and feel, do and observe the following exercise with at least one partner. One or more of you should be watching, and one or more of you should be working.

Size and Speed Exercise

If you are watching: Call out the instructions; and as the actors who are working move, notice how it looks like they feel as they do the movement.

If you are working: Simply follow the physical instructions without trying to do anything more than you are asked, but notice how the Sizes and Speeds make you feel as you perform the instructions.

- Start walking around the rehearsal space at what feels to you like the most neutral, *Medium* quality for you to move. Deliberately try to say nothing with the way that you are walking. (The person giving instructions should wait until this neutral quality has been established before going on.)

- Now, start walking as *Big* and *Fast* as you can. This should not look dancelike; it should be a way you would actually walk down the street, but as Big and Fast as you can make it.

- Now, keep your walking *Fast,* but make it as *Small* as you can, until you are as Small and Fast as you can be.

- Now, keep your walking *Small,* but make it as *Slow* as you can, until you are as Small and Slow as you can be.

- Now, keep your walking *Slow,* but make it as *Big* as you can, until you are as Big and Slow as you can be.

- Now return your walking to a Medium size and a Medium speed.

- Switch functions, and do it again.

What did you see? Have a conversation about how the people working seemed to feel in each Size and Speed, and how you felt as you did the exercise. Did people seem nervous or excited when they were Small and Fast? Confident when they were Big and Slow? Aggressive or happy when they were Big and Fast? Sad or introspective when they were Small and Slow? These reactions are common with these Sizes and Speeds. Did you experience any of these feelings (or others) when you performed the exercise? The point is not to rely on Sizes and Speeds to make you feel a certain way, but also not to deny that committing specifically with your body often increases what you do feel and express in a given moment.

Sizes and Speeds combined with specific movements are an extremely potent storytelling device. To demonstrate this point in class, I ask an actor to perform the following directions:

> Enter the room Big and Fast, with your focus outside of yourself, smiling and looking around. When you get to the center of the room, stop and look down suddenly at a spot about six feet in front of you and stop smiling. Become very Small and Slow with your body, and still staring at the spot, walk slowly toward it.

Before the actor comes in the room, I tell everyone else the "story": She is coming in to surprise her best friend for his birthday, but finds the friend lying unconscious on the floor. Invariably, if the actor follows the physical directions exactly, the audience "sees" the frightening scenario even though the actor has no idea what it is! That is how much your audience will work for you if you are specific and committed with your movements.

During an audition, it is easy to doubt yourself and "pull back" physically. Pulling back is never helpful to your performance because it gives your monologue a predictable sameness that can make it seem uncommitted and unsuspenseful. When you've chosen and rehearsed clear, specific staging using Sizes and Speeds, your body has something to grab on to when you audition, which is a relief when you're under pressure.

"The Death of Medium"

How did it look when the actors returned to Medium at the end of the Size and Speed exercise? How did it feel when you did it? All of the Big, Small, Slow, and Fast combinations look so specific that I immediately start imagining scenarios to go along with them: a bunch of office workers racing to meet a deadline, vacationers at a resort, people at a funeral, and so on. When the actors go back to Medium, the picture immediately flattens and it doesn't look to me like any kind of situation in particular.

From here on, we're going to proceed under the principle that, when you are staging your monologue, your movements will be either Big or Small, Slow or Fast. Period. No Medium. This principle helps you commit physically to your staging choices and rids you of the habit of holding back during performances.

Don't worry that committing to Sizes and Speeds will make your movements cartoonlike. The point is to find *your* Big, yo*ur* Small, *your* Slow, and *your* Fast, so that you can express your staging clearly. In some cases you'll need to be willing to work beyond your comfort zone, especially if you have a fear of being "too big" or "too theatrical." To encourage yourself, watch the work of bold, expressive actors, and study how they naturally use Sizes and Speeds in their performances without going over the top.

Choosing Sizes and Speeds for Your Descriptions

Assign Sizes and Speeds to your Descriptions. The choices are

- Big and Fast

- Small and Fast

- Small and Slow

- Big and Slow, *and*

- Any one of the Sizes and Speeds *becoming* another Size and Speed

These last can be used for "builds" of Size and Speed within a Chunk. I used two builds for the Alma monologue.

When choosing Sizes and Speeds for each of your Descriptions

- *Choose them quickly, based on the descriptive words:* For example, is "frustratedly lectures" Big or Small? Slow or Fast? Go through all the Descriptions, choosing a Size and a Speed for each one.

- *Adjust your choices so you don't have the same Size and Speed combination twice in a row.* Changing Size and Speed on each Chunk makes your staging suspenseful. If you have the feeling that two Chunks in a row should be "Slow and Small," ask yourself which Description is faster or bigger, and change the Size or Speed accordingly.

- *Make sure you have variety.* For example, if your Sizes and Speeds are mostly Small—or mostly Slow—mix them up some more.

Section	Chunk	Description	Size and Speed
Beginning	You needn't try to comfort me. I haven't come here on any but equal terms	Nervously scolds	Small and Fast
	You said, let's talk truthfully. Well, let's do! Unsparingly, truthfully, even shamelessly, then!	Resolutely challenges	Small and Fast to Big and Slow
Middle	It's no longer a secret that I love you. It never was. I loved you as long ago as the time I asked you to read the stone angel's name with your fingers.	Bravely confesses	Big and Slow
	Yes, I remember the long afternoons of our childhood, when I had to stay indoors to practice my music—and heard your playmates calling you, "Johnny, Johnny!" How it went through me, just to hear your name called!	Bitterly complains	Small and Slow
	And how I—rushed to the window to watch you jump the porch railing! I stood at a distance, halfway down the block, only to keep in sight of your torn red sweater, racing about the vacant lot you played in.	Excitedly confides	Small and Fast
	Yes, it had begun that early, this affliction of love, and has never let go of me since, but kept on growing. I've lived next door to you all the days of my life, a weak and divided person who stood in adoring awe of your singleness, of your strength.	Frustratedly lectures	Big and Slow to Big and Fast
	And that is my story! Now I wish *you* would tell *me*—	Abruptly regroups	Small and Fast
End	**[Climax:] why didn't it happen between us? Why did I fail?**	Agitatedly demands	Big and Fast
	Why did you come almost close enough—and no closer?	Brokenly begs	Big and Slow

- *If you are using builds:* You can, if you like, have the Size and Speed in the Chunk *before* the build be the same as the one that *starts* the build. Similarly, you can have the Size and Speed *after* the build be the same one that *ends* it. Use a build only once or twice in a monologue—more than that can get repetitive.

Refer to the following checklists as you make choices for the Chunks, Descriptions, and Sizes and Speeds of your monologue. When you're ready, go on to the next chapters, which are about combining these choices with other directing elements in order to create your staging.

Checklist for Making Choices

You have chosen Chunks for your monologue that

- ❑ Don't overlap your beginning, middle, end structure
- ❑ Feel like distinct units to you
- ❑ Are of different lengths
- ❑ Are not too many or too few (probably 7–10)
- ❑ Define the climax as its own Chunk

You have chosen Descriptions for your Chunks that

- ❑ Are seeable adverbs and verbs
- ❑ Suggest a vivid picture for each Chunk
- ❑ Contain no plot
- ❑ Have words used only once for this monologue
- ❑ Have variety
- ❑ Add up to a complete Story

You have chosen Sizes and Speeds for your Descriptions that

- ❑ Are not repeated twice in a row
- ❑ Have variety

CHAPTER 3

STAGING OPTIONS

Staging can make or break an entire production. It can make the play flat, repetitive and tedious to watch—or dynamic, suspenseful, flowing, and beautiful. Good staging honors the writing and makes the story the star. It feels good to the actors because it reassures them that the story moves forward and flows so that they don't have to push with their acting to keep the audience's attention. You can create good staging for your monologue by making specific and unique choices about how and when you use your body to stage each of your Descriptions.

In this chapter, I discuss the many options you have to choose from when staging a monologue. In chapter 4, I show you a possible staging for Alma's monologue. Keep your own monologue in mind as you work through this chapter, then apply the choices and examples in chapter 4 to create your own staging.

The Square: Your Stage

For the purpose of staging your monologue, work in a perfect square, six feet by six feet. The square provides you with a "stage" to act on. The square is designed to orient you in any audition space, and to contain the overall movement in your monologue. Maintaining the size of your square is important. Working with a larger square than six feet by six feet makes your monologue seem "all over the place." Your square, however, can be smaller if you audition in a room too small to place a six foot square. To get used to working in the square, mark it with objects or tape on the floor of your rehearsal space.

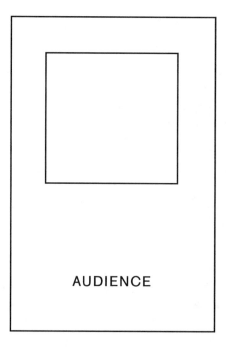

AUDIENCE

When you first work with the square, you may feel a bit confined, especially if you have long legs. That response is normal. Practice walking with smaller steps to get from position to position. Watch another actor perform the examples below and notice that it doesn't look like he is confined. Instead, it looks like he is sure of where he is going, and his movements look sharp and clear.

Where you place the square in the audition room is crucial: the downstage edge of your square should always be a comfortable distance from those who audition you so they never feel like you are on top of them and so they are able to watch you freely as an audience would. With one or more other actors, experiment in different sized rooms with what would feel too close to the auditors. Make a habit of always placing the downstage edge of the square behind the point that is too close to them. Beginning this habit now and practicing it prepares you to orient yourself easily in an audition room of any size.

The square should always be away from the walls of the room you are working in, even if that means making the square smaller. If you test it out, you'll see that, when an actor is hugging the walls on the sides or the back, he seems to disappear.

Focus

In a play, using the element of *focus* means attracting the audience's attention to what the director wants them to look at any particular moment. In an audition, of course, your audience will always focus right on you. Choosing the focus for a monologue therefore means deciding where *you're* going to focus when you perform it. The focus you choose for a monologue audition should

- Allow you to be seen as much as possible throughout the performancc

- Make absolutely clear who your character is talking to

Usually, your auditors do not want you to "use" them, meaning to look at them and act with them in your audition. In most cases they want to be free to watch you as an audience would. Therefore I suggest you always *not* use them, unless you are specifically asked to do so.

Choosing Your Focus

What are the choices for where you will focus? In your monologue, the character may be

- Talking to one other character

- Talking to one other character but referring to someone or something else in the room

- Talking to two or more characters

- Talking to a crowd

- Talking directly to the audience

A soliloquy is a monologue in which the character is alone on stage. In a soliloquy, the character may be

- Talking to himself

- Talking to someone who is not there

- Talking to God (or "the gods")

For monologues in which your character is talking directly to one other character, take your focus up to a point at or slightly below your own eye level, as if the other character is standing directly centered behind the auditors. Have someone watch you and help you find the focus spot that lets them most see you. Focusing too high or too low makes it hard to see what is going on with you as you act the piece. Keep this focus (or any other you may select from the options to follow) while you stage your monologue so that you become used to it.

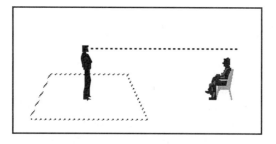

When you move during this kind of monologue, it is important for your focus spot to stay in the same place. If you change focus as you move, you are cheating your auditors out of seeing you perform full on, and potentially confusing them by making it look like the other character is moving around as you move.

It is also vital to establish the habit of *never looking down* at the floor during any part of your monologue unless it is absolutely part of your Story—for example, if your character is actually referring to something or someone on the floor. Looking down unspecifically can take your audience out of the Story by making it seem as if you've forgotten your lines or staging. If you choose to show with your focus that your character is thinking or remembering something for a moment, always look up: your audience will stay with you no matter what.

A monologue in which the character is talking directly to one other character is the most common choice for auditions. Adjusting the focus for other kinds of monologues is simple:

• If your character is talking to multiple people, such as to a courtroom or other gathering, simply let your focus expand a couple of feet to either side of the center point as if there are more people standing behind the auditors. Monologues meant to be addressed directly to the audience, however, usually work best if you focus them as if to one person.

• For soliloquies, in which the character is talking to himself (as in *Hamlet*), think about how you would "talk to yourself" in a room alone. Your focus would probably roam around, never resting on any one place for very long. The only other focus adjustment to make for a soliloquy is to make sure you are seen as much as possible. Therefore, always turn out toward your audience; let your focus roam, but keep it at or above eye level at all times. This practice lets your audience "see you thinking."

• If your character is talking to God, or to "the gods", experiment with referring up with your eyes only—not your head— during the monologue.

• Monologues taking place on the telephone can be performed by holding or miming a phone. Make sure you can be seen at all times, and keep your eyes at or above eye level as in a soliloquy.

• In certain monologues, you may need to place the focus on something in the square with you. An actor in my class once worked on a soliloquy in which the character was alone in a room, talking both to herself and to a phone which she begged to ring with a call from the man in her life. The actor placed the "phone" (she didn't actually use any props) as if it were on a small table in the upstage left corner of her acting area, and she looked at that place during appropriate places in the monologue. The rest of the monologue was focused as for a soliloquy.

• Sometimes your character talks directly to another character and also refers to someone or something else that is outside the square. In Phebe's monologue to Silvius in *As You Like It,* she refers repeatedly to Rosalind, who has just exited. To make this clear, you would place the focus for Silvius in the usual place behind the auditors, because he is the character to whom the monologue is addressed. You would place the focus for the exited Rosalind at a downstage diagonal (right or left) from you. Then, in your staging, you would decide when Phebe should look at Silvius, and when she should look to where Rosalind has exited.

Use your common sense when it comes to choosing the focus for a monologue. The priorities are that you are seen as much as possible by the auditors and that the Story is told simply and without confusion from any changes in focus. If you are unsure, have a friend stand in for you and direct her to try different choices of focus until you have the effect you want.

Placement Options

I now examine *placement* inside the square and how different places you stand in it might affect your audience. Divide your square so that you end up with nine potential positions:

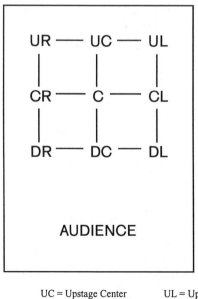

UR = Upstage Right	UC = Upstage Center	UL = Upstage Left
CR = Centerstage Right	C = Centerstage	CL = Centerstage Left
DR = Downstage Right	DC = Downstage Center	DL = Downstage Left

Switching functions back and forth with another actor, try out the following positions.

- If you are functioning as the actor, place your focus behind the audience at your own eye level as you stand in each position. Notice how each position feels to you as an actor.
- If you are functioning as the audience, notice how the actor affects you when she stands in each position.

Start with the actor in the Upstage Center of the square:

The actor moves to Centerstage:

And now to the Downstage Center:

Does the actor feel too close to the audience? If so, move the square back, or if the room demands, make it smaller.

Now try Upstage Right, Centerstage Right, and Downstage Right:

And Upstage Left, Centerstage Left, and Downstage Left:

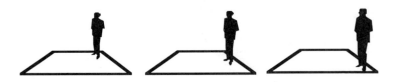

How did each position feel to you as the audience? How did it feel as an actor? Following are some qualities I've noticed about each position and some possibilities for their use in your staging.

- *Upstage Center* is a strong, balanced position that can seem removed or commanding, depending on your interpretation. Notice as an audience member that, when the actor starts from this position, it looks like she can now "go anywhere." For this reason, it's a strong place to start your monologue.

- *Centerstage* is a place you can use to call attention to important parts of your story by literally "taking centerstage." If you don't have much movement in your piece, you can stand here for much of it while easily keeping the audience focused on the story. It is also a very balanced place to start your monologue.

- *Downstage Center* is closest to the audience. It can be confrontational or vulnerable, depending on how it is used. It's a great place to use to bring out your Climax. Downstage Center should be used sparingly—too much and the audience may start to feel uncomfortable, and/or the position can lose its power. Because of its intensity, you should seldom start your monologue here; doing so gives you no place to go unless you back up from it very soon after starting.

- *Upstage Right and Upstage Left* can have a lurking, suspicious, or hesitant quality that you might want for the beginning of your monologue; like Upstage Center, both positions give you somewhere to go. Because they are close to the audience and off to the side, both positions tend not to work well as places to start your monologue unless you have a specific reason to do so.

- *Centerstage Right* and *Centerstage Left* are good for transitional moments between stronger Chunks, and for ending up in for a few moments to make a point. They're usually not strong places to start. If you compare starting in them to starting in any of the upstage positions, you'll notice how much weaker they seem.

- *Downstage Right* and *Downstage Left* are not as confrontational or as vulnerable as Downstage Center, but they can be used for making strong statements in the monologue. They are often strong places to be immediately before the Climax of your monologue, if you choose to put it Downstage Center. I do not suggest starting your monologue in either of these positions unless you have a specific reason to do so.

To ensure that your staging is always strong and clear, it is important for now to make a commitment to these nine positions—not anywhere in between. Doing so also helps you memorize your staging. Try standing in between two of the positions: notice how it's not as clear a choice as one of the nine basic positions.

When you use the positions in the square to stage your monologue, your audience has no idea the square is there. They see just the result of committing to the positions: clean, committed staging. When you act your monologue fully, it will naturally take some of the "edges" off the staging, so don't worry that you will look like you are moving around on a chess board.

Movement Options

Often, out of fear, actors have little or no *movement* in their monologue auditions. Or the movement they do have makes them self-conscious when performing because it is not specific enough—the movement doesn't make sense to their bodies. Many are also concerned about having too much movement in their monologues. My answer is that movement in and of itself is neither good nor bad; it really has to do with telling the Story. Use as much movement as you need, fully performed. I think you would agree that it is as undesirable to have a great deal of general, unfocused movement as it is to stand in one place with a restricted feeling. Some monologues support a lot of movement; other monologues have language so intricate or so powerful that they're served best by economical movement.

Let's look at some movements in the square that you may want to use in your staging. Only a few examples are provided—there are many more that you can come up with yourself and experiment with. Trying these examples with one or more other actors helps you start to develop an awareness of how movements in the square look to your audience.

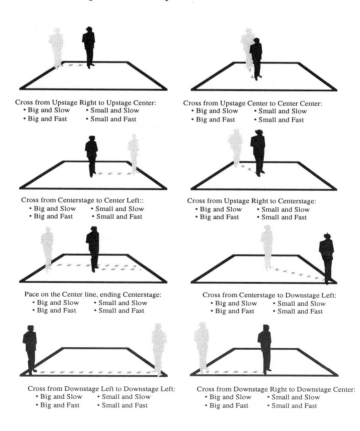

Cross from Upstage Right to Upstage Center:
• Big and Slow   • Small and Slow
• Big and Fast   • Small and Fast

Cross from Upstage Center to Center Center:
• Big and Slow   • Small and Slow
• Big and Fast   • Small and Fast

Cross from Centerstage to Center Left::
• Big and Slow   • Small and Slow
• Big and Fast   • Small and Fast

Cross from Upstage Right to Centerstage:
• Big and Slow   • Small and Slow
• Big and Fast   • Small and Fast

Pace on the Center line, ending Centerstage:
• Big and Slow   • Small and Slow
• Big and Fast   • Small and Fast

Cross from Centerstage to Downstage Left:
• Big and Slow   • Small and Slow
• Big and Fast   • Small and Fast

Cross from Downstage Left to Downstage Left:
• Big and Slow   • Small and Slow
• Big and Fast   • Small and Fast

Cross from Downstage Right to Downstage Center:
• Big and Slow   • Small and Slow
• Big and Fast   • Small and Fast

At first, you, as the actor working, should keep your focus at your own eye level, above the seated audience. Later, you can try the same movements with the different kinds of focus you might choose for a soliloquy or for a monologue addressed to multiple people. The actor watching should take note of how each movement looks from the audience's perspective. The actor watching can also suggest different movements to try in the square. Try the same movements with the different Sizes and Speeds, too, and notice the effects. Come up with your own movements in the square and try them with different Sizes and Speeds.

Gesture

Gestures are specific choices for your upper body—your arms, hands, and sometimes even your facial expressions—that can be used as needed to stage your Descriptions. In chapter 4, I suggest you actually set gestures in your staging, separately from the acting. Doing so has two major advantages:

- It ensures that your staging tells your Story.

- It gives your *whole body* something specific to do when you audition that you can use fully as an actor.

Your first thought when you read this might be "But what if I want to act the monologue differently in the moments of the performance?" The answer is that any gesture can be acted many different ways. To experience what I mean by this, try the following gesture combined with a line:

Throw your hands up in the air, shaking your head, and say, "What was I thinking?" Do this very mechanically, with no inflection or expression.

Now do it with a

- Begging quality

- Joking quality

- Demanding quality

- Teasing quality

- Lecturing quality

As you can see, the gesture remains roughly the same, but the way it's done by an actor working in the moment can vary infinitely. This is a demonstration of how free you are to act your monologue once it's specifically staged. Throwing your hands up in the air and shaking your head for that small Chunk of text might be the way you would stage a Description like "helplessly surrenders." Notice that once the Description has become physical staging, only the movement remains. The actor doesn't need to *act* "helplessly surrenders" at all. The actor can now simply *use* that specific movement to express her impulse in the moment.

Setting the gesture means not waiting until you feel like it to commit to your monologue with your body. When you read and practice the acting approach for monologues in part 2, you will see how much I advocate that the moment can mean anything you need it to mean as an actor. And when you learn to combine your staging with your acting in chapter 7, you will experience for yourself and see in your partners how dynamic and truthful your monologue can be when you act it fully using your specific staging. You'll have what actors in a well-staged play have: a reliable structure with which to act the piece fully.

Setting the gestures does not mean you'll be waving your arms around during the entire monologue. Keeping your hands and arms still for a particular Chunk is also a choice. Waving your arms around the whole time *and* restraining all gesture by tensely or lifelessly keeping your arms at your sides are two sides of the same coin: they're general and show a lack of commitment in the acting *and* in the directing.

When you stage, give yourself permission to choose gestures that absolutely get your Descriptions across. I encourage you to let the gestures be bigger for now than you might feel comfortable with as a performer, even if it feels false or even "indicated" to you. As you get used to committing with the gestures, you'll start to make them your own, to make them ways in which you are fully expressing yourself. Anything that finally feels too big can be taken down once you've completed your staging.

Budgeting

In the next chapter, I discuss how to *budget* your choices of placement, movement, and gesture to tell your Story. Budgeting helps you maintain the suspense in your monologue and is exactly what it sounds like: you decide when you're going to "spend" a movement, gesture or placement choice in your staging, so that you guarantee each staged Description is unique and doesn't look like any other. It also keeps you from using choices too early that you want to save for later on.

Just as you should avoid using the same Description word, and the same Size and Speed twice, so should you avoid repetition of the same kind of placement, movement, or gesture unless it is a deliberate choice, or unless you're using it in a specifically different way. If you moved on every Chunk, or if you gestured similarly, or if you kept going back to the same place in your square, each would lose its specificity and meaning. Budget your staging elements so that you can decide the most effective places to use them.

Staging Guidelines

Using specific choices about your focus, placement, movement, gesture and budgeting combined with your Sizes and Speeds helps you stage each Description of your monologue fully and clearly. The following staging guidelines are what I have found to be most effective about 90 percent of the time. None of them is an absolute rule—each can be "broken" for a specific reason to bring across an effect you want in your staging. Refer to them when you are staging your monologue.

- Most monologues work best when you start them from the Upstage Center, Centerstage, or Upstage Right position in the square. These positions all give you somewhere to go.

- Most climaxes are clearest if they are Centerstage or Downstage Center.

- Unless you have a specific reason to do otherwise, always move to one of the nine positions in the square.

- Work with the least number of movements—actual traveling

in the square—required to get your Story across. Always move for a reason.

- Your overall movement in most cases should progress down-stage as the monologue continues. Backing up or turning around and moving upstage during your staging can work well, but always have a specific reason for doing so. Otherwise, it might feel to your audience like you are backtracking or starting over.

- Don't move on more than two Chunks in a row unless you have a reason. More movement than this gets repetitive and starts to kill the suspense.

- Movement usually works best if you go only half a square's length at a time (for example, Upstage Center to Centerstage instead of all the way to Downstage Center in one move).

- *Balance* your staging in the square by keeping track of when you have gone to the Right or the Left sides. The next time you want to go to the side, go Right if you went Left before, and go Left if you went Right before.

- If you choose to turn your back on the audience to walk up-stage, make it the briefest time possible so they don't lose you. Raise your voice so you can be heard, and let them see your face again as soon as possible.

- Never look down during your monologue unless your char-acter is actually looking down at something in the square with her. If you do choose to look down, do so for the least time needed to get the idea across.

- If your character refers for a moment to something outside the square, place it at a downstage diagonal so that the audi-ence gets a three-quarters view of you rather than a profile view. This will keep your audience with you.

- If you pace from side to side, keep your head up and your eyes on your focus point the whole time to keep the audience with you.

- Break the rules! Any guideline can be broken for a reason (as you will see I have done in my staging for the last Chunk of Alma's monologue). You may put a large, pacing circle into your staging. You may throw up your arms and twirl around all over the square. You may decide only to take two small steps downstage for your whole monologue. What's most important is that you make each choice deliberately because it's the best way you can think of to stage a particular Description.

About Props

It is wonderfully theatrical when an actor enters a room and tells a complete story using only himself. For this reason, I suggest you use props only when absolutely necessary. If you use a prop, make it something you can easily handle, such as a letter or a photograph you can keep in a pocket (especially if you are auditioning with more than one monologue). Your audition should never be about the props you are using, and getting props out should never take up audition time. Telephone monologues are fine if they are well written and compelling to watch, but I personally don't care if actors actually use phones or just mime them. Use your common sense about props: simplify or omit them as much as possible, and consider the purpose of the audition when deciding if props are appropriate.

Checklist for Staging Options

❑ You have practiced placing the square in the room, making sure to place it behind the point that is too close to the auditors.

❑ You have chosen the focus appropriate for your monologue.

❑ You have experimented with the placement options in the square with a partner, noticing how each position affects the audience.

❑ You have experimented with the movement options in the square using different Sizes and Speeds, noticing how each movement affects the audience.

CHAPTER 4

STAGING YOUR MONOLOGUE

Unless a monologue specifically demands otherwise in the writing, I recommend you first stage all monologues on your feet—without a chair. You're most expressive when you're using your whole body, and performing your monologue on your feet shows you move with ease on stage and commit fully to your choices—vital qualities for auditions. After you have staged a monologue on your feet, you can always "take it down" in size and perform it in a chair if you need to. In chapter 7 I show you how you to perform a fully staged monologue in a chair while keeping your specific choices in place.

In order to stage effectively, you must have your lines perfectly learned, word for word. Not only does paraphrasing insult the writing, it wastes energy because you never really learn the line and have to spend time remembering it. You should also memorize where your Chunks begin and end.

As you stage for the first time, remember to keep your directing separate from your acting. Concentrate only on the directing so that you can learn how much of the story you can tell purely with staging. As you stage, you will probably have some acting impulses, just as any actor would in a rehearsal with a director. Note them, but keep going back to your Descriptions for your staging choices.

Bring a sense of play to your staging, especially the gesture. Be prepared to make bold, fun choices that will absolutely get your Descriptions across. The actor in you may cringe at some of them at first; they may feel false or indicated. Let them. In the chapter 7 I show you how adding the Action to your staging naturally makes your staging more motivated and real. Any movement that still feels too big can be adjusted. I've found that 90 percent of the time, what feels too big to an actor is not too big to those watching. Audiences love commitment and theatricality.

Warm up your voice and body before you stage. Rehearse with a full, supported stage voice so that you won't have to think about it later when you perform your monologue.

When you stage, keep a chart of your current choices, as I do in this book. Later you can refer to it when you are rehearsing a monologue you haven't worked on for a while.

Planning Your Staging

Before you start to stage your monologue, I suggest you first plan some movement and placement choices by working backward—from the end of the monologue to the beginning. Planning helps you start to budget, so you don't use up all your options too early. Answer the questions below for your monologue. Here I provide my initial choices for Alma's monologue:

- *Where do I want the character to be at the end?* Because I feel Alma builds in strength until the end of the monologue, I want her to be Downstage Center at the end. The staging leading up to it can tell how she gets there. (However, I ended up adjusting this choice slightly, as you will see later.) Downstage Center means she's as close as she can be to the audience; this spot feels most confrontational.

- *Where do I want the character to be for the climax (if the climax comes before the end)?* Also Downstage Center, for the same reasons.

- *Where do I want the character to start?* At the Upstage Center position in the square. Upstage, because the very first Description is "nervously scolds"—she's not rushing into her confrontation right away. This placement creates distance between Alma and John. A lot happens in this monologue, and I want to save the positions farther Downstage for later. I'm having her start Upstage *Center* because Center is stronger and more balanced than Left or Right and this monologue is definitely a show of strength for Alma.

- *Based on the words in my Descriptions and my interpretation of the Story, in which Chunks do I definitely want the character to move? Or, which Chunks could really use some movement (combined with Size and Speed) to get the Description across?* On the second Chunk, "resolutely challenges": I think I will have her move forward to Centerstage.

On the fourth Chunk, "bitterly complains": I think I will have her move to the Centerstage Left position. Moving to the side will help communicate that Alma is changing her tactic to a less confrontational one in this Description.

On the fifth Chunk, "excitedly confides": Here I can have her move to the Downstage Left corner. Moving closer to John helps stage the word "confides," and the fast Speed will help communicate "excitedly." I'm having her move Downstage Left here because I'm saving Downstage Center for the climax and the end.

On the eighth Chunk (the climax), "agitatedly demands": Here she will move Downstage Center.

- *Now refer to the staging guidelines in chapter 3.* If you compare my answers to the guidelines you will see I have satisfied many of them. Again, however, you don't have to follow these guidelines exactly every time; you only need to consider them and make sure that, if you break one, you break it for a reason. I did break the "always move to one of the nine positions in the square" guideline, as you will see below.

As you can see, I've already made the major movement choices for Alma's monologue. Answering these questions helps me see the whole Story in terms of the movement, and keeps me from "painting myself into a corner" by running out of movement choices before I've reached the climax and end. It's also likely that some of these choices will change. But change is what is fun about staging—you get ideas while planning, but you always get better ones while you work with them. Your answers to these questions, along with the staging guidelines in chapter 3, give you ideas to start with when beginning to stage your monologue.

The First Moment: Countdown

To address the first moment of any monologue, I introduce the *Countdown*. The Countdown is used in three ways in this book:

- To give you a consistent starting place for your first Chunk of staging

- To start yourself in the acting exercises in part 2, so that you can practice being present and truthful from the very first moment when you act your monologue

- To start your monologue when you audition

In an audition, the Countdown helps you make a clean transition from introducing yourself into the first moment of your monologue. To see this for yourself, try the Countdown with a partner:

- Center yourself in the square (when you have staged your monologue, you will always do the Countdown from the position in which you have chosen to start the first Chunk of your monologue). Your posture should be straight, but without straining. Your knees should be unlocked, your arms relaxed at your sides, and (very important) you should be breathing freely.

- Introduce yourself. Look at your partner and say "Hello, I'm _____, and I'll be doing a monologue from _____."

- Now, maintaining your posture and your breathing, simply look at a spot on the floor that is about 5 feet in front of you. Look down *only with your eyes*—do not drop or hang your head.

- Slowly and silently count down "3...2...1...GO." At GO, look up over your partner's head to your chosen focus spot. This is when you begin the first moment of your monologue.

The Countdown shows auditors several important things about you:

- You are prepared (and therefore dependable, professional, and mature).

- You won't waste their time (and are therefore considerate and easy to work with).

- You come to performances ready to go (and therefore you start acting the second the lights go up instead of halfway through the scene; you don't "warm up on stage").

The Countdown is based on a simple fact: there is *nothing* that you can do or say to yourself the second before you audition that will make the monologue better or that will make you feel better about performing it. Your emotion may very well be terror, and there is nothing you can do to change that; what you *can* do is commit to the work you have put into your monologue and trust it will come across. (If it doesn't go quite the way you would like, by the end of this book you will know how to work on it specifically and fix it in your next rehearsal.) Practice the Countdown and use it from now on when you stage your monologue or do any of the upcoming acting exercises. As you get used to doing it, you may be surprised to find how comforting it can be to have this simple habit to replace all those moments of second-guessing yourself.

When I introduce the Countdown in class, I usually ask people to demonstrate the *worst* examples they can come up with of actors who come into the audition room, then spend many moments preparing—even doing vocal warm-ups, then perhaps do two or three half-starts of their monologues before finally continuing. Try this yourself with a partner—come up with your own examples of poor entrances. Then try entering and starting your monologues with the Countdown. Put yourself in the place of a director looking for reliable, professional actors. What do actors communicate about themselves simply by how they start their monologues?

Staging

Now let's go back to the beginning of Alma's monologue and stage the Description for each Chunk. Notice as I work how using the Sizes and Speeds, along with placement, movement, and gesture makes each Description vivid and distinct.

I suggest you read this section over and note which factors could also influence your own staging decisions. Then apply the same sort of process to your monologue.

It's ideal—but not essential—for you to stage with a partner in the room the first time through. (Remember: you won't focus on your partner anymore—use the focus choice you made in chapter 3). Your partner can help you test your staging by telling you if all of your choices are coming across.

As you stage your monologue, your goal should be to communicate the Descriptions for each Chunk with physical movements *only*—no acting.

BEGINNING SECTION, FIRST CHUNK

Chunk	Description	Size and Speed
You needn't try to comfort me. I haven't come here on any but equal terms	Nervously scolds	Small and Fast

Placement

Upstage Center, the same place I would start the Countdown

Movement

For the reasons I describe above in "Planning your Staging," Alma is going to stay in this position.

Gesture

What does "nervously scolds" look like? "Nervously" might mean tense shoulders and arms, with even a little trembling in the hands. "Scolds" could actually mean shaking a finger at John once or twice. The restricted arms, the slightly shaking hands, then the finger raised to scold should all have a Small and Fast quality to them.

Test the Staging

When you have staged your first Chunk, test it. This is best done with a partner who has your directing chart—a copy of your Chunks, Descriptions, and Sizes and Speeds in front of him. As you stage, he can record your choices. To test the staging:

• Start with a Countdown.

• On the GO of the Countdown, bring your eyes up to your focus point; then silently perform the staging you have chosen for your first Chunk. A silent performance lets your partner see if you have fully staged your Description. Ask your partner if he saw both words in your Description, and your Size and Speed. If you were working on Alma's monologue he might answer, "I saw 'scolds,' but I didn't see 'nervously,' and it was more Small and Slow than Small and Fast." Then you would need to work on it some more. If he did see everything, you would go on.

• Now test your staging aloud. Do your Countdown; look up to your focus; and say the line(s) of the Chunk as you do the staging. The point here is not to "act" the lines—or the Descriptions—at all. Nor do you want to artificially make your voice into a monotone. You're simply adding the words so that you can check the timing of the movement and gesture. Let your voice simply go along with what your body is doing; let your body lead. If you have a Chunk that is Big and Fast and very active, let your voice be affected by what your body is doing, but don't try to act the lines in a certain way.

• Work on the timing. Find out how much of your gestures you need to do to communicate each Description simply and vividly. You don't necessarily have to do the gesture all the way through each Chunk. A little bit could be enough. Work on your timing until you get a sense of the words, movement, and gesture coming together. This experience is very subjective. Your timing should feel right to you, and look clear to someone watching. When you're ready, go on and stage the next Chunk.

BEGINNING SECTION, SECOND CHUNK

Chunk	Description	Size and Speed
You said, let's talk truthfully. Well, let's do! Unsparingly, truthfully, even shamelessly, then!	Resolutely challenges	Small and Fast to Big and Slow

Placement and Movement

As I decided before, on this Chunk Alma will move to Centerstage, building from Small and Slow to Big and Fast. This dramatic change in Size and Speed during the Chunk will show "resolutely." Moving to the strong Centerstage position, staying focused on John, will show "challenges."

Gesture

I don't think any gesture is needed to get this Description across; the movement says it all.

Test the Staging *and* the Transitions

The transitions between the Chunks of staging are a full part of the staging. In fact, they are *just as important as the staging for the Chunks themselves.* If an actor "drops out" between each Chunk—doesn't stay active and make a clear distinction between the changes in gesture, movement, and Size and Speed from one Chunk to another—the staging looks vague and messy, and all the hard work put into telling the Story is lost.

To make your transitions clear:

- Stay active. Don't drop out physically after each Chunk.

- Decide what you are going to do to get from one Chunk to the next, and set it. For example, if Alma "nervously scolds," I might decide to have her deliberately lower her hand at the end of the line ("on any but equal terms").

Just as you did with the first Chunk, test the second one silently and then with the words. Then test the whole thing: the Countdown, the first Chunk, the transition, and the second Chunk. Can your partner still see the Description of each Chunk? Does the timing look and feel good? Are you staying active in the transition?

After you've tested and perhaps adjusted what you have so far, go on.

MIDDLE SECTION, THIRD CHUNK

Chunk	Description	Size and Speed
It's no longer a secret that I love you. It never was. I loved you as long ago as the time I asked you to read the stone angel's name with your fingers.	Bravely confesses	Big and Slow

Placement and Movement

Alma stays Centerstage, but she becomes Big and Slow. I think these choices show "bravely."

Gesture

For "confesses," she can make a Big, Slow gesture toward him with both hands.

Test the Staging and the Transitions

Again, test this staging and each transition silently, then with the words. Then go back to the beginning and test all the staging you have so far.

MIDDLE SECTION, FOURTH CHUNK

Chunk	Description	Size and Speed
Yes, I remember the long afternoons of our childhood, when I had to stay indoors to practice my music—and heard your playmates calling you, "Johnny, Johnny!" How it went through me, just to hear your name called!	Bitterly complains	Small and Slow

Placement and Movement

Alma moves to the Centerstage Left position.

Gesture

"Complains" can come across if we see Alma shake her head slowly as she crosses to her left. I think "bitterly" will also come across as she gets smaller in size. Perhaps "bitterly" can also come into her face, a "sour" expression. Remember: I'm going all the way with gestures for now. I would experiment with the timing of this gesture to see how much would make "bitter" come across, and how much would be too much. Remember that, when the monologue is performed, all gestures and facial expressions can change a little or a lot, depending on the moment.

Test the Staging and the Transitions

MIDDLE SECTION, FIFTH CHUNK

Chunk	Description	Size and Speed
And how I—rushed to the window to watch you jump the porch railing! I stood at a distance, halfway down the block, only to keep in sight of your torn red sweater, racing about the vacant lot you played in.	Excitedly confides	Small and Fast

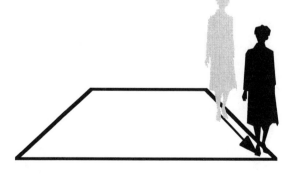

Placement and Movement

I particularly like the Description for this Chunk because it gives Alma some variety from the heaviness and pain implied in most of the monologue. "Excitedly confides" lets us see how she felt about John as a young girl, which to me makes the rest of the monologue even more dramatic and moving.

I'm having Alma move immediately here, Small and Fast, to Downstage Left. This timing contrasts well with the moves she has done so far, which have looked more calculated.

Gesture

For "excitedly," I want her actually to smile here. Again, this is how specific I believe you can get with gesture. If a smile is always in the staging, it ensures that this Chunk always helps add variety to the monologue. *How* she smiles is up to the actor playing Alma when she acts the monologue (smiles can look like anything from ecstatic to furious). For "confides", I'm having her lean forward slightly toward John when she finishes her move to Downstage Left.

Test the Staging and the Transitions

MIDDLE SECTION, SIXTH CHUNK

Chunk	Description	Size and Speed
Yes, it had begun that early, this afflicion of love, and has never let go of me since, but kept on growing. I've lived next door to you all the days of my life, a weak and divided person who stood in adoring awe of your singleness, of your strength.	Frustratedly lectures	Big and Slow to Big and Fast

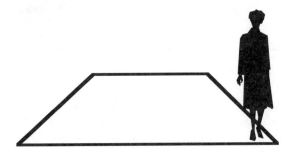

Placement and Movement

Alma is going to stay Downstage Left for this Chunk. When you stay in one place for several Chunks in a row, as Alma does in this monologue, it is especially important to make sure you perform your Size and Speeds fully.

Gesture

"Lectures" is a vivid word that can be communicated with a "lecturing" gesture, using one or both hands. Doing the gesture with the Size and Speed build will show "frustratedly."

Test the Staging and the Transitions

MIDDLE SECTION, SEVENTH CHUNK

Chunk	Description	Size and Speed
And that is my story! Now I wish *you* would tell *me*—	Abruptly regroups	Small and Fast

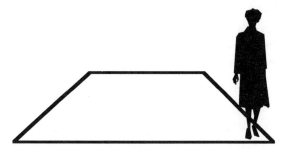

Placement and Movement

I'm going have Alma stay Downstage Left for this short Chunk, in preparation for the climax.

Gesture

For "abruptly regroups," I'm going to have Alma quickly and deliberately stop her "lecturing" gesture from the last Chunk by clenching her fists. A bold gesture like this one helps build the suspense before the climax.

Test the Staging and the Transitions

END SECTION, EIGHTH CHUNK (AND CLIMAX)

Chunk	Description	Size and Speed
[Climax:] why didn't it happen between us? Why did I fail?	Agitatedly demands	Big and Fast

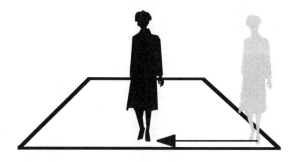

Placement and Movement

Now, after the buildup of suspense, Alma finally comes to Downstage Center to ask her big question in the climax of the monologue. The Size and Speed is Big and Fast, which shows "agitatedly" and helps show "demands."

Gesture

Further, for "demands," I'm going to have her keep her fists clenched and reach sharply forward with her arms.

Test the Staging and the Transitions

END SECTION, NINTH CHUNK

Chunk	Description	Size and Speed
Why did you come almost close enough—and no closer?	Brokenly begs	Big and Slow

Placement and Movement

Here I break the guideline that says "always move to one of the nine positions in the square" by having Alma take one Slow step backward. After the bold movements she has made so far, this is the best way I can think of to show "brokenly." To this point, she's only increased or maintained her closeness to John. Now, she's finally giving up her ground.

This staging communicates my interpretation that, at this point, Alma knows she's lost John. In addition, by taking a step back into the square, Alma now seems completely alone. This movement also happens to counterpoint the line she's saying: "almost close enough—and no closer."

Gesture

I'm going to have her "beg" just slightly with her arms. Doing so Big and Slow combined with the step backward helps emphasize "brokenly."

Test the Staging and the Transitions

The Last Moment

Even though I've completed the staging for this monologue, *it's not over yet!* If the actor playing Alma were to suddenly "pop" out of the last moment of her monologue, it would be very jarring to those watching. If she were to "drop" out lifelessly after so much specific work, it would be disappointing.

Instead, treat the last moment of a monologue with care by doing the following:

- Hold the last moment for a "reverse Countdown" of "1...2...3."

- On 3, become Big and Slow with your body, and *put* (don't flop) your arms down to your sides as you slowly "float" your attention down from your focus spot to make eye contact with the auditors. Doing this tells them the performance is over. Don't look down before looking at the auditors. (Transitioning to another monologue, if you are performing two or more in one audition, is covered in chapter 8.)

Holding the last moment, then deliberately coming out of the monologue, treats you, your performance and your audience with respect. This practice lets everyone adjust to the monologue being over. It also encourages you to treat your performance positively, which I discuss in detail later on.

Making Changes

As I staged Alma's monologue, I changed many of my original choices. I changed several of the elements I had to work with, including Descriptions, Sizes and Speeds, movements and gestures. I even changed the climax. As you stage your monologue, expect many of your initial choices to change too.

I found the "right" choices for my interpretation of Alma's monologue because I started with *a* choice. This happens every time I direct something. I'll have a great idea at home, but it invariably changes in the rehearsal room. Making changes never means that any preparation or thought you put into your monologue is wasted. From the first moment you start to work on any piece, you are making an investment in it. That investment may pay off in an unexpected way, but isn't that part of the fun of what we do? If we could stage or act perfectly the first time, it wouldn't be as exciting or as satisfying.

Rehearsing Your Staging

When you have completed your staging, continue to rehearse it, making adjustments until all of it feels clear and specific to you. Make sure you are clearly changing your Sizes and Speeds according to your choices; don't let them even out after all of the work you have put in. Make sure all your transitions are active, and that you always hold the last moment.

Rehearse until you have your staging completely memorized. It's thrilling to watch an actor who knows the staging of his monologue inside and out; he is free to use every specific movement to express what is happening in the moment when he acts it. Drill your staging until your body knows exactly what it is doing in each moment.

Forget the Descriptions

When you have memorized your staging, *let go of the words in your Descriptions!* Instead of keeping the adverbs and verbs in your mind, let your *body* remember the movements you chose to express them. Doing so is very important, because if you rely on "acting" your Descriptions to get them across, your staging will be less specific and your acting will seem preplanned instead of true in the moment.

Use the checklist below with a partner to test all of your staging once it is completed. When you are able to perform all of your staging from start to finish without any hesitation, you are ready to use it in chapter 7, when you finally combine the directing with the acting of your monologue.

Checklist for Staging Your Monologue

Preparing to Stage

❑ You have chosen where you are going to focus in the monologue.

❑ You have set your square.

❑ You have memorized your lines cold. You have memorized where your Chunks begin and end.

❑ You have answered the "Planning Your Staging" questions for your monologue.

Staging

❑ You have created staging for each Chunk of your monologue.

❑ Each Chunk of your staging contains the adverb and verb in your Description and your Size and Speed.

❑ You have staged clear transitions between the Chunks.

Testing Your Overall Staging

❑ You are starting with a Countdown.

❑ Your focus is consistent throughout the staging.

❑ Your voice is full and supported throughout the staging.

❑ All of your Sizes and Speeds are absolutely clear.

❑ You are not looking down during the monologue unless it is a specific staging choice.

❑ Each gesture is specific and unique to the monologue.

❑ All of your transitions are active.

❑ The overall movement is balanced in the square.

❑ Unless you have a specific reason, the overall movement comes forward (downstage) during your monologue.

❑ Unless you have a specific reason, you are not moving on more than two Chunks in a row.

❑ The climax is clear.

❑ You are sustaining the last moment.

After Staging

❑ You've recorded your final staging in your chart.

❑ Your staging is completely memorized—you can perform it from beginning to end without stopping.

PART 2
Acting Your Monologue

CHAPTER 5

ACTING IN THE MOMENT

If a director's job is to stage the story, the actor's is to live the individual, unique moments that arise each time the story is performed. An actor's strength, therefore, lies in being fully present and dealing with what is *really happening* in a performance. When we go to the theater we often see performances that seem completely preplanned, predictable, and stale. We sometimes are lucky enough, however, to see performances by actors who know how to act *in the moment*. Their performances have a bold, spontaneous and truthful quality that keep us on the edge of our seats.

In this chapter, and in chapter 6, I want you to concentrate only on acting your monologue truthfully in the moment, which means that you should put aside all of your work as a director, including your staging. In part 1, the actor in you "stayed out of the way" while you made bold, specific directing choices for your staging. Now let your work be about playing and experimenting with your monologue as an actor without letting the director in you worry about what it looks like. Very soon, in chapter 7, you'll put your directing and your acting back together.

The reason separating the directing from the acting of your monologue is so effective is that, once you have taken responsibility for all of the structure and staging as a director, you can trust that the Story is being told and therefore be completely free of "directing yourself on stage" while you act. By this I mean the experience we've all had while acting of listening to the voice in our heads that says, "Do it like *this*. Say the line like *that*." This voice is the "internal director." This internal director's instincts are often excellent, but its place is in rehearsal when staging choices are being made. When you listen to the voice in performance, you are "out of the moment" with your attention uncomfortably on yourself; and guess what, you're not really acting anymore.

Because you know you are putting a great deal of detail and specificity into staging the Story of your monologue as a director, you as an actor are free to experiment with allowing yourself to do *anything* needed in the moment on behalf of your character based on some simple choices you'll make.

As I discussed in "How to Use This Book," the acting exercises in these chapters are based on the technique of Practical Aesthetics. I've found this technique ideal for acting audition monologues for several reasons.

- Practical Aesthetics gives you one simple objective, called an *Action,* to play for your monologue.

- An Action doesn't require you to be in a particular emotional state in order for you to perform it. You will learn how to make it important to you, but you will not have the impossible task of trying to make yourself feel a certain way before you audition.

- Practical Aesthetics makes a distinction between the character and the actor. If an actor embraces the fact that she cannot actually *become* the character—*especially* in a two minute monologue—she is then free to "act on the character's behalf" by bringing *her* entire personality to the Action. When combined with staging, acting on the character's behalf creates a compelling *illusion* of the character for the audience.

- When adapted for audition monologues, the technique powerfully addresses two practical questions: "Who do I act with?" and "How can I act truthfully without other actors to play off of?"

- To work, the technique requires risk taking and bravery on the part of an actor, which make his monologues thrilling and enjoyable both to perform and to watch.

The Action

Central to many acting techniques is the practice of having one Action (objective, goal) for a scene. In Practical Aesthetics, we define the Action as "your goal on stage," so that it is always personal to you. After you choose an Action for your monologue, you can then let each line mean anything it needs to mean for you to achieve the Action.

If you refer to *A Practical Handbook for the Actor,* you will see that there are several qualities that an Action should have. These qualities include being specific and fun to perform, and having a test in another person.

For the purpose of this book, I provide a list of tried-and-true Actions that already have these qualities. The Actions listed are grouped roughly by type so that you can choose milder or stronger versions of the same idea.

To get* what I deserve
To get what's owed me
To get an apology

To lay down the law
To get someone** to play
   by my rules
To teach a simple lesson
To teach an important lesson
To teach a serious lesson

To get someone off his ass
To get someone to grow up
To get somone to stand on her
   own two feet
To get the truth
To get a confession
To get a straight answer

To get a favor
To get help
To get someone to bail me out
To get someone to rescue me

To sell a great idea
To get someone to seize a great
   opportunity
To get someone to take a chance/
   risk
To get someone to rise to the

To get someone to put her faith in me
To get a chance
To get another chance
To get a fair shot

To get forgiveness
To get reassurance
To get a promise
To get a commitment
To get an ironclad guarantee

To put someone in his place
To knock somone off her high horse
To burst someone's bubble

To get a break
To get someone to bend the rules
   for me

To get someone to join forces
   with me
To win an ally
To get someone to come through
   for me

To clear up a terrible
   misunderstanding
To clear up a simple
   misunderstanding
To clear up a silly misunderstanding

challenge

To get someone to take a dare

To make a deal

To get a compromise

To get someone to meet me half way

To make a truce

To get someone to accept my help

To get someone to take my hand

To prevent a terrible mistake

To make someone do the right thing

To make someone take responsibility

To make someone hold up her end of the deal

To make someone face the facts

To wake someone up to the truth

To smack somone into reality

To get someone to let his hair down

To get someone to accept a treat

To get someone to accept a gift

* Wherever you see the verb "to get" feel free to substitute a more specific verb if you like, such as "convince," "beg," or "force."

**The word "someone" is used here, to leave the choice of relationship, like "a loved one," "a friend," "an enemy," "a jerk," up to you. The relationship should not reiterate the actual relationship in the monologue but should describe its essence; for example, the character's father could be "a loved one," "a rival," or "a buddy." Use the relationship only if it helps you. I've found much of the time it's the specific goal in the Action, not the relationship, that helps an actor most compellingly play the scene.

Notice that none of these Actions requires you to be in any kind of emotional state in order to begin performing it. Under the pressure of an audition, it is impossible to control how you feel. Having an Action that doesn't rely on your feeling a certain way to do it gives you something to do when you *don't* feel like it. As you work with Actions in this chapter, note that all kinds of emotions *are* engendered in you as you pursue an Action in the moment. These emotions occur naturally because of the difficulty in achieving the Action, not because you are trying to make yourself feel a certain way. Therefore, the emotions and moments you experience as you pursue the Action are always truthful.

You can also trust that, once you have picked an effective Action for your monologue, any emotion or moment it generates in you *does* belong in the monologue (so you won't have to

direct or edit yourself while you are performing it). This principle applies especially to emotions or moments that make you
feel uncomfortable—they are the natural result of picking a
challenging Action. Playing them fully makes your monologue
performance risky and dynamic. If you are unfamiliar with
working this way, try it and see how it works for you. You may
find that you feel freer and more truthful as an actor and that
you want to bring this way of working into the rest of your
acting.

Choosing an Action

In chapter 1, you answered a series of introductory questions as
part of your directing preparation. Your answer to "What does
the character want the other character(s) to do as a result of
hearing this monologue?" also helps you choose an effective
Action for your monologue.

The Action is *how* you're going to get the character what he
wants. If, for example, you're working on one of George's monologues from act 2 of *Who's Afraid of Virginia Woolf?*, you might
decide he wants Martha to realize their marriage has been a
complete sham. To act on his behalf, you might choose the Action "to smack someone into reality." If you think he should go
about it in a gentler way, you might choose the Action "to teach
a serious lesson."

Read your monologue a few times, thinking about what your
character wants the other character(s) to do. Which Actions on
the list could get your character what she wants? You can also
modify the Actions (see the notes under the list) or use varia-
tions of these ideas to come up with your own.

In the introductory questions in chapter 1, I decided that what
Alma wants is for John to choose her instead of Nellie. Two
Actions that could help get Alma what she wants are "to beg for
another chance" and "to force someone to take responsibility."
Imagine how different each of these Actions would make the
effect of Alma's monologue. There are many other Actions that
could work well too. So how do I decide which Action would
work best for my interpretation?

In answering the introductory questions, I also recognized
that this scene is one of the last in the play and that it is Alma's
final chance to win John. In examining what has happened in

the play to this point, I also noticed she has decided to change—to be more like him—to win him. I think a good Action would be "to get someone to rise to the challenge."

If an actor performs Alma's monologue with that Action, it might look like Alma is saying, "I've changed into what you wanted, so I challenge you to follow through." I'm also choosing this strong Action instead of "to beg for another chance." This choice of strength helps play against the fact that my directorial interpretation of the monologue is that Alma fails in the end. The actor playing Alma needs something to keep striving for. The fact that the direction (and the line "Why did I fail?") already dictates that Alma loses John makes it even more heartbreaking that she is still trying. I didn't choose an Action like "to force someone to take responsibility" because that is basically what Alma has been trying to get John to do throughout the play, and it has only driven him farther away from her. "To get someone to rise to the challenge" is a new, positive tactic to get him to change his mind.

If you're torn between very different choices of Action for your monologue, keep in mind that the playwright has already taken care of the conflict. Ask yourself which Action would help your character to *create order* in the scene; which Action would be the *surest* way to get your character what he wants. Attempt to bring order to your monologue with your choice of Action, and let the playwright throw you off in the lines. You will feel freer as an actor and those moments when the lines contradict your Action will be exciting to perform and to watch.

If you are working on a monologue not from a play, screenplay, or other fully realized story, use your common sense, your instincts, and any clues the writer has given you about what the character wants in order to choose an effective Action.

For soliloquies in which the character is talking to himself, ask, "What does the character want *himself* to do". Then choose an Action that will accomplish it. For example, in act 3, scene 1 of *Hamlet* ("To be, or not to be"), Hamlet may want himself to realize his present circumstance is better than facing death; or, instead, he may want to encourage himself to take action. In these examples, the actor could use the Action "to prevent a terrible mistake" or "to inspire a friend to take a risk," respectively.

Finally, when you're choosing Actions, don't be afraid to play against the text! Characters aren't always direct about what they want in their lines, so don't test an Action by looking for a number of lines to support it. Only a few lines may support the Action. Sometimes I ask actors to experiment by choosing the Action that seems *least* likely for the piece and trying it first to open them up to the possibility of playing the monologue quite differently from the way they'd originally thought. This experimental thinking helps them start to let the moments mean anything. Working with an Action that lets you go after what the character wants in a less obvious way often brings a refreshing, unexpected quality to a monologue.

To start experimenting with this freedom for yourself, try acting your monologue with different Actions using the exercises that follow. Then decide on the one that feels best for your interpretation. Note, however, that it is better to commit to one Action than to try and discard so many that you never allow one Action to become habitual in your rehearsals.

The As-If

An *As-If* is a simple device you use to explain exactly what a particular Action means *to you.* It provides you with a personal "text" with which to practice the Action. The As-If is a current or easily accepted scenario from your own life in which you would want to accomplish the Action you have chosen for your monologue.

We all do As-Ifs. Who does not have hundreds of conversations in his head every day? These conversations usually start something like, "I will not allow you to humiliate me in front of the family anymore." or "I've worked here for two years, and it's finally time I got that promotion" or "We've been working too hard—let's go on a great vacation!"

As-Ifs come from our fantasy lives, from what we would love to say to someone or wish we had the guts to say but can't, for whatever reason. I'll bet you've already had many As-If conversations in your head today. They are the what-if conversations we suggest to ourselves. "What if he started another untrue rumor about me and I finally told him off?" "What if I had to ask my parents for more money to stay in school?" "What if she mistakenly thought I was trying to steal her boyfriend?"

Like Actions, As-Ifs work most effectively for monologues

when they have certain qualities. Good As-Ifs

- *Explain what the Action means to you, but do not parallel the relationship or the circumstances of the monologue.* This quality is sometimes hard for actors to understand until they've tried it and seen how strong the results are. You've already interpreted the monologue with the choice of Action, and using an As-If that duplicates the circumstances destroys that carefully chosen specificity by *reiterating* the monologue rather than *interpreting* it. If you were working on one of George's monologue from *Who's Afraid of Virginia Woolf?,* and if you'd chosen the Action "to teach a serious lesson," you would perhaps use an As-If like "it's as if I'm teaching my little brother he has to stop hanging around with the dangerous crowd at school" or any other "serious lesson" important to you. Not "it's as if I'm getting my wife/ girlfriend to see that our relationship isn't working," because that's what the monologue itself is about. The writer has already written the story. The As-If needs to support the Action you've chosen so that you are free to pursue it in a way meaningful *to you.* Don't worry about whether the text makes sense—it does. When you perform it, it seems the character cares as much about what he is saying as you do about your As-If. Having an As-If that parallels the circumstances in the text, however, restricts your acting of the monologue: some part of you always compares the two, and you are less likely to take chances.

- *Are from a present or possible future situation in your life— not from the past.* Acting is about the present moment, and choosing a past situation for your As-If limits your possibilities in the moment because you already know how it was resolved, making your monologue lose the "anything can happen" quality that is so compelling to watch. Instead, listen to the conversations you have in your imagination that start with "What if."

- *Specifically define exactly what you want the person in your As-If to do now (apologize, give you the money, commit to a dinner date, etc.).* This quality gives you an immediate test of how close you are to getting what you want in the As-If. If the test is too vague, like "I'm getting my sister to be nicer to me," your acting in the moment is also vague. Change it to

"I'm getting my sister to agree not to argue with me during the holiday." This specificity provides you at any moment with a yes or no answer to act on.

- *Are things you really want to do or really must do.* Don't choose pain-in-the-ass "chore" As-Ifs that aren't fun to do (like getting your roommate to pay the phone bill on time). A good As-If makes your heart beat a little faster and makes your body a little restless when you think of it. Let your body tell you whether you want to do the As-If or not. A good guideline for As-Ifs is that they should be so fun you *can't wait* to do them, or so important you *must do them now.* They're also a great opportunity to indulge yourself in the fantasy of acting on things you may not be able to act on in real life.

- *Are scenarios you can easily accept.* While they *can* be about your fantasy of telling off your brother-in-law, even if you wouldn't in real life, As-Ifs that are too fictional, and too hard to accept, won't be as accessible. "It's as if I were the President of the United States" is likely to run out on you because you would have to keep creating that fantasy. Most good As-Ifs come from relationships and circumstances that already mean a great deal to you.

- *Are not about life-and-death circumstances or about people in immediate physical danger.* These situations can shut you down because they are *too* emotionally loaded.

- *Challenge you because you don't know whether you'll get them or not.* Your As-If shouldn't be too easy, but it should also not be impossible to achieve.

- *Should always be addressed to another person, never to yourself.* Doing an As-If to yourself only makes you self-conscious. Even if your monologue is a soliloquy, make the As-If about someone else. If your monologue is addressed to a group, or to the audience, you can still practice the Action with an As-If that is about one person.

- *Should not be about show business!* As-Ifs for audition monologues should be about personal situations you care about in your own life. As-Ifs about getting ahead in the business serve only to remind you of your audition and make you self-conscious.

As you can see, finding As-Ifs that work for you is a personal process. I've found the best way to come up with an As-If is to suggest the Action to yourself with your eyes closed. Ask yourself, "Who would I need to 'get a big favor' from?" (or whatever the Action is), and see which faces and situations pop into your mind. Then make the situation specific so that you know why it's important and why you would act on it now.

Refer back to these guidelines as you try different Actions for your monologue. Use the As-If exercises below to try them out so you can decide which Action and As-If works best for you.

Acting the Action

The As-If exercise that follows is a kind of role-playing exercise, like asking your friend to pretend he's your boss so you can practice asking for a raise. The only difference is that your partner will be silent so you can practice working alone in response to his attitudes. This exercise must be done with another person, even if he's not an actor—all he has to do is sit silently and give you his attention. Note that your partner does not have to be the same gender as the person in your As-If.

You and your partner should agree before starting the exercise that you have the freedom to say anything you wish, and that neither of you will take any of it personally. It might seem obvious that since you will be pretending he's someone else, your partner shouldn't take it personally; but as you will be working off what you perceive are his responses, you need to set this agreement between you.

To start playing your Action truthfully from the very first moment, use the Countdown from chapter 3. But instead of looking up at the wall, for now look directly at your partner on the GO of the Countdown so that you receive a live response from him to base your impulses on. (In the next chapter, you'll learn to act just as fully with your focus up above your partner.)

When you use the Countdown to start the coming exercises, make a habit of continuing with the exercise for at least thirty seconds, *no matter what*—even if it's confusing or you think it's not going well—to help break the habit of judging and apologizing for your work as you are doing it. Continuing can be very hard to do at first. However, it will help you learn the incredibly valuable skill of staying with the moment and not sentencing the monologue (and yourself) to death for "bad starts." In an audition, continuing shows your auditors that you are able to stick with—and save—a scene that may have started off shakily. Starting over in your rehearsals, or asking to start over in an audition, prevents you from building that skill and from gaining the self-confidence it gives you. Make it a point of pride *never* to start over.

The As-If Exercise

- Stand in the center of your rehearsal space facing your partner, who should be sitting in a chair. *For the partner: You need only give the actor your attention by looking at her the whole time she is working. You will not speak, nor will you try to respond in any particular way. If you smile or change your position slightly, fine. The point is neither to try to do anything nor to try to suppress anything.*

- First, simply look at your partner from the point of view of the Action. If the Action is "to make a deal," notice how close or how far it looks like he is from wanting to make a deal with you. What is his mood? Is he uncomfortable? Open? Happy? Notice how easy it is to endow your partner's responses when you look at him from the specific point of view of the Action.

- Now, imagine specifically how your partner would look if he *were* willing to give you what you want in the Action. This image is the *"cap"* of the Action. At any moment, you can look at your partner and gauge how close to or how far away from the cap he is.

- Do a Countdown. When you get to the GO, look directly at your partner. Take in his attitude, and begin speaking to him in a full, supported voice, as if he is the person in your As-If scenario. Use the name of the person in your As-If. Immediately ask for what you want in the As-If. For example, if your Action is "to teach a serious lesson," you might say, "Brian, I don't want you to go to that party because you've got to stop hanging around with the wrong crowd at school."

- Pause a moment and notice the response. How did asking for what you want change your partner? What do you need to say to him now? Say it: "I know how tempting it is to want to be popular by doing things that are dangerous." What is his response? "Don't laugh; it's not funny. I don't want anything to happen to you." Notice that in your responses you are sticking to the Action—teaching the lesson—while changing your tactics in response to what your partner is *actually doing*.

- Keep going. Practice changing your tactics in order to change your partner, and notice each time whether it gets you closer to or farther from the cap of your Action. Stay in the moment with what is really happening between the two of you.

- When you first do this exercise, stand in one place, even if you have the desire to get closer to your partner or to touch him. Express these impulses instead by how you talk to him, your facial expressions, your gestures, your tone of voice. Doing so makes you stronger and more expressive, because you aren't relying on the crutch of physical proximity or physical contact to reach your partner.

- After you are used to the exercise, experiment with moving on your impulses. Without getting too near to your partner or touching him, let yourself move boldly and clearly on the impulses you get from working off of him. See if committing to the impulse with your whole body and voice makes it easier to change him.

Once you accept your partner's responses as what you have to act on, it is a lot of fun to do this exercise. Some people get stuck at first: "But that isn't how the person in my As-If would respond." The point is not to *believe* your partner is your brother but to pursue the Action *as if* you're talking to your brother; your partner's responses are what you actually have to deal with.

When you are able to sustain your As-If and your attention on your partner for several minutes, becoming completely engrossed in how he is changing from moment to moment and how you are able to make him change, you are ready for the next exercise.

Acting the Action with the Lines

You must have the lines of your monologue memorized *abso-*

lutely cold for this exercise. You should know them by rote, with no particular line readings rehearsed in.

• Use the Countdown as before, and start your As-If. When you feel connected to the Action and to your partner's responses, *simply substitute the lines of your monologue for the words of your As-If.* In other words, you are still trying to accomplish the Action, and the only thing that should change about what you're doing is the *words you happen to be using.* Continue for at least thirty seconds, no matter how strange it may feel.

• What happened? Did pursuing the Action with the lines of your monologue feel roughly the same as when you were pursuing the Action with your As-If? Were you acting on what you were really getting from your partner? Or did you find yourself suddenly acting the monologue in a preplanned way?

• Try again. The goal in this work is to let the lines mean *anything* they need to mean in the moment in order to get your Action. It makes no difference which words you happen to be using, yours or the writer's, even if the writer's words contradict what you mean in the moment.

• Go back and forth between your As-If words and the lines of your monologue. Go back into your As-If the minute you feel yourself losing the connection to your Action or partner, and pick up where you left off in your monologue as soon as you have the connection back. See if you can gently take your attention off "how it sounds" and put it back on the Action.

• Let yourself gesture freely in this phase of the exercise. Practice getting your partner to change by using your whole body.

• Take turns practicing the exercise and watching each other work. See if you can feel in yourself and see in your partner any moments when either of you starts acting in a preplanned way rather than simply pursuing the Action.

Actors watching others do this work for the first time are usually thrilled by how truthful and heartfelt the monologues become. They experience how much an audience is dying to see actors who take risks and tell the truth, and how satisfying it is for the audience when they do.

The lines of your monologue will become "your own" because you are saying them from a deeply invested part of *yourself,* a part you accessed with the As-If. That deeply invested you is *much* more fascinating to watch than any idea of "the character" your mind could have invented. The audience will see the result—that the character seems as invested as you are in the lines—and be drawn into the story as it unfolds in the moment. Practice the exercises until you can go all the way through the lines of your monologue from start to finish while fully pursuing your Action with your partner.

Let the Lines Mean *Anything*

When we were first taught how to work this way in school, we were encouraged (by a playwright!) to "let the words be gibberish." Not to make the lines mean nothing, but to let them mean *anything.* (Think about how many meanings there could be for the line "I love you.") In some acting approaches, actors are asked to write out a complete "subtext" for their characters (i.e., decide what the character really means by what he says). The actor is then asked to memorize this subtext along with the lines. My opinion is that this approach is about "planning the moment." Instead, trust your interpretation as an actor—your choice of Action—and let the moment fall where it may as you pursue your Action fully. In this way, the subtext—what your character really means—becomes a continual and truthful surprise for you and for your audience.

Connection

Pursuing your Action using your As-If or using the words of the monologue requires that you connect to what is really going on in your partner. Sometimes in the beginning an actor makes the mistake of doing her As-If or monologue "at" her partner instead of connecting *to* him. True connection requires you to give up all expectation of what is going to happen and simply address yourself to what really *is* happening. Your task is the Action, and you are much more likely to "win an ally" if you connect to what your partner is "asking" you to do with his attitude than you are if you try to force him, which will probably only make him resist you. When you are the partner who is silent in the exercises, notice: Is the active partner really connecting to you? Or is she just talking "at" you?

As you build your connection in the As-If, *keep it* as you transition into the lines of your monologue by continuing to work off your partner's behavior. If you lose your connection, go back into your As-If to get it back. Practice until you can get all the way through your monologue while staying connected to your partner.

Breathe!

Keep checking in with your breathing as you work in the moment. It's an incredibly common habit for actors to hold onto their breath in an attempt to stay in control because of their uncertainty or nervousness about the risks they're taking with the As-If. Breathing deeply lets you take in what is really happening with your partner and gives you the breath to express your impulses immediately and fully with your voice.

More about Staying in the Moment

In scene classes, I do not let actors stop the scene if they lose a line. They have to stay focused on their Action and their scene partner until the line comes back, even if it takes until the end of the class. The wonderful result is that everyone always has their lines cold; and a beautiful, mature habit of staying focused and concentrated develops when an occasional line is lost. It's also surprising how quickly the lines come back when the actor commits to staying in the scene. If you drop a line and are in the habit of not letting it throw you, but of making that moment *part* of the scene, more often than not the audience will not even notice, or will go to the intermission saying, "Did you see that incredible moment between them?"

Exactly the same goes for moments you think you've gotten "wrong" in your monologue. When you are acting a monologue, you are the least qualified person to tell how it is going because you are inside it. Often the moments that feel wrong to you feel that way because you are experiencing the natural discomfort of doing something bold or risky or vulnerable. So many times in acting classes an actor will have an uncomfortable time in a scene or monologue and begin to apologize for it, only to get the comment from everyone that it was some of her strongest work. Becoming a mature, focused actor means leaving it up to the audience to think what they will about your work—you won't judge it for them.

To help you build the habit of staying in the moment, I suggest embracing the idea that, once you've begun a scene or monologue, there is *no moment* until you've finished that is *not* the scene, *no moment* that is *not* a part of the story you're telling for the next several minutes. This includes losing lines, thinking what you've just done is stupid, huge jolts of inspiration, or a glass accidentally falling off a table. Your acting will immediately get stronger if you let go of trying to make your performance "right" and allow it to be what it *is*. Watch an actor express the thought "I have no idea what I'm doing—I'm totally lost right now" *with her line,* and you will be surprised by how perfect it seems for the monologue because it is the truth of the moment while that actor is pursuing the Action. Taking the leap from your Countdown into truthfully playing whatever is happening in the first moment, then the next, then the next as you pursue your Action is how you can practice the brave quality of "staying in."

The Last Moment

The last moment of your monologue needs the same commitment to staying in as the rest of your monologue. Actors often back off of the last moment of a monologue by dropping out as soon as they've said the last line, especially if they've been feeling frustrated or vulnerable in their performance. Most likely, however, these difficult moments have been engendered by the Action, and are a very important part of the story. That uncomfortable last moment can be beautiful and moving if you commit to it.

No matter what is happening, stay in the last moment of your monologue, still playing your Action for a moment or two *after* the last line, and practice deliberately coming out of it. The "reverse Countdown" in chapter 4 supports this practice in your staging. Don't cheat your audience out of the last moment of your monologue. Hold your last moment, no matter *what*.

Checklist for Acting in the Moment

❑ You have chosen an Action for your monologue, based on what your character wants from the other character(s) he is addressing in the monologue.

❑ You have chosen an As-If that explains that Action to you.

❑ You have practiced the Action with your partner, using your As-If.

❑ You have practiced the Action with your partner, using the lines of your monologue.

❑ You are able to pursue your Action as freely and as spontaneously with the lines of your monologue as you are able to with the words of your As-If.

❑ You are able to start from your Countdown and pursue your Action all the way through your monologue without stopping, no matter what.

CHAPTER 6

WHO DO I ACT WITH?

Now I address what many actors feel is the most challenging part of auditioning with monologues: acting them without focusing on a partner. In this chapter you'll learn to embrace this challenge and make it work for you. Once you understand and practice some simple changes in the As-If exercise from chapter 5, you'll find you can act your monologue just as fully without a partner as you can with one.

The immediate question I hear when I introduce this material is, "If I'm not focusing on my partner, then where do I get my impulses *from?*" The answer is in the As-If.

We all have As-If conversations our heads all the time. We imagine talking to people we know or people we expect to encounter. And when we have these conversations, we also imagine the other people's responses, based on how we just "talked" to them in our heads. I'm sure you've had an imaginary conversation at one time or another something like this one:

You

I need Friday the 24th off. I have to be in my best friend's wedding.

Boss

I need you on Fridays.

You

This is important to me. I've been working overtime for you and I'd really appreciate it if you could return the favor. I have to be there Friday morning.

Boss

I'm sorry, but you'll have to come to work that day.

You

Please, can't someone else come in?

Boss

No.

You

That's not fair. I'm giving you plenty of notice, and I never ask for time off. You let other people off on Fridays, and I do more work around there than anyone.

Boss

That's exactly why I need you to stay.

You

Don't you realize if you treat people unfairly, they're going to quit? This is so important to me that I might have to quit if you don't give me the day off.

Boss

I don't want you to quit, but I need you that Friday.

You

Maybe we can work it out. What if I work overtime that Thursday?...

In chapter 5, when you learned to use your As-If to work off your partner, you had to take risks in order to change him. In the example above, notice how you unhesitatingly took risks to change your boss—you even threatened to quit. You determinedly kept changing your tactics as your boss changed his in your imaginary conversation. You didn't have to invent his responses; your mind automatically suggested them. The key to acting your monologue without focusing on your partner is to work off of your own imagination, just as you do in the conversations you have in your head every day.

Acting with Your Focus Up

Although you will not be focusing directly on your partner anymore, you still need him in the room with you for this exercise. All he has to do now, however, is watch. He has become your audience, providing you with the performance atmosphere you need to effectively rehearse your monologue.

To start, remind yourself of the focus point you chose for your staging. For a monologue addressed to one person, focus at or a little below your own eye level, as if there is someone standing just behind your partner. When you work on other kinds of monologues, follow the suggestions of focus described in chapter 3.

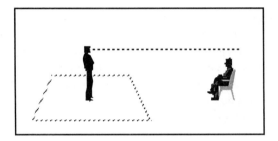

- Do a Countdown. On the GO, look up to your focus point. Keep your attention there for the entire exercise.

- Start speaking to the person in your As-If. Ask for exactly what you want right away. In the above example, you would say, "I need Friday the 24th off."

- What was the response? *Take a risk* by going with your *first impulse* and respond to your As-If person.

- Continue, keeping a sense of play about the exercise. If you get stuck, *take a risk:* remind yourself of the cap of your Action, and notice how close you are to getting it. Ask what the response is. You'll always get an answer back.

- Let yourself gesture boldly and freely as you perform the exercise. Express yourself with your whole body. Make sure you are using your voice fully.

- The next step, as in chapter 5, is simply to substitute the lines of your monologue for your As-If. If you get lost or distracted, *stay in* and work through it, taking risks with how you say the lines of your monologue, based on your impulses, in order to achieve your Action.

It's important to keep a sense of experimentation as you do this exercise. Let the moments of your monologue mean anything they need to mean. The goal is the same as when you first tried the As-If exercise in chapter 5: that you pursue your Action as fully with the lines of your monologue as you do with your As-If.

Most people find acting their As-If with their focus up easy to do. Some even find it easier than working off of a live partner. The key is going with your first impulses as to what your As-If person's response are in each moment.

To clear up a common misunderstanding, you do not have to waste energy trying to "see" the face of the other person on the wall! You will never consistently be able to do this, and trying to do so will distract you from pursuing your Action. The As-If person's responses come from inside you, just as they do when you are having a conversation in your mind as you walk down the street. All you have to do is keep your focus up as you are having the conversation and it will *look* like you are talking to another person. The process is the same if you are working on a soliloquy or on a monologue that addresses more than one other character: you still keep the As-If person in your head; the place on which you are visually focusing is the only thing that changes, creating the illusion that the character is talking to himself or to multiple people.

In his book *True and False: Heresy and Common Sense for the Actor* (1997), David Mamet points out that the mind will rebel if asked to *believe* something that is not happening, but it is always ready to *accept* any scenario it might find interesting to imagine at the moment. In the As-If fantasies we all have every day, we accept the scenarios without question so that we can entertain ourselves by mentally acting on them. For example, I can instantly have fun imagining I have won a million dollars and fantasizing about what I will do with it. If, however, I try to make myself believe the money is actually in my hands, my mind rebels because I know it's not true. The same goes for the As-If person's presence. Don't waste your time trying to believe she is there or trying to "see" her. Simply accept her presence, just as you automatically do in your everyday fantasies.

The skill you're developing by accepting the presence of your As-If person is working off of your own energy as you pursue an Action. There's no one acting but you. Your partner's presence is simply creating a performance atmosphere, which gives you the pressure to keep going. The commitment you make and the risks you take in changing the As-If person make the lines of your monologue come alive.

Acting this way is a lot like playing tennis or handball with yourself against a wall: If you hit the ball so that it comes back to you easily, it's going to get boring really soon (like staying within a preplanned performance and taking no risks). If you slam it so hard out of recklessness or frustration, so hard that you'll never be able to get the ball back, the game's over (like "going over the top" emotionally by forgetting your Action and what you want in your As-If. If you do this, you won't be telling the story anymore, just indulging the emotion). But, if you hit the ball just hard enough so that you have to run a little in order to return it, you remain true to your goal: to make the game fun and a little unpredictable by taking risks.

It's empowering to realize *you* are in charge of generating the energy of your monologue. You are able to keep going, no matter what the circumstances. The paradox is that you control the impetus for your monologue by voluntarily *giving up* control of the moment, letting the imagined person's response *tell* you what you need to do next. Recognizing and building this skill—of keeping yourself going by committing your energy and taking risks—makes your monologues fun and challenging for you and entertaining for your audience. Audiences are smart. They can tell when an actor is playing it safe. If you don't know what's going to happen next but stay true to your Action by playing your impulses fully, your audience will be drawn into watching you play each new moment.

Checklist for Who Do I Act With?

❑ You are able to pursue your Action fully, with your focus up, with the As-If.

❑ You are able to pursue your Action fully, with your focus up, with the lines of the monologue.

CHAPTER 7

ACTING YOUR STAGING

The class combining acting and directing is an exciting one in the monologue workshop, because we get to see everyone's work come together. If you've done all the work in this book until now, you have everything you need for a great monologue performance: solid staging and the ability to act fully in the moment without a partner. Now you're ready to pursue your Action fully *with* your staging.

In this step, we get to see the staging of your monologue collide head-on with the moments that are generated by the Action. As in a good production, this combination creates a performance consistent in its overall shape but engaging, connected, and spontaneous in its individual moments. To accomplish this to its greatest potential, both your staging and your acting in the moment need to be strong. If either is weak, one of the following will be the result.

- When your staging is clear and dynamic but your acting is general because you aren't fully pursuing your Action, or because you don't have a specific, important As-If, your performance looks mechanical. Your acting is not alive and connected to the moment.

- When your staging is not suspenseful (vague, repetitive movement or gesture, no differences in Size and Speed) but your acting is strong and committed, your overall performance seems "all over the place," overacted, or strained because you're trying to compensate for your lack of direction. Performances of your monologue in this case are also inconsistent.

Don't cheat yourself and your audience out of exciting performances of your monologue! Do the following preparation with a partner. Watch your partner to see the difference between just *doing* the staging and *acting* the staging. If you need to change anything to make either your staging or your acting stronger, do it before going on.

- Warm up, vocally and physically.

- Go through the mechanics of your staging aloud several times, making sure it's completely memorized. Ask your partner to give you feedback about whether your staging includes specific movements and gestures and clear Sizes and Speeds. Watch your partner do his staging and give him the same feedback.

- Now, put the staging aside and practice the Action with the As-If with your focus up, allowing yourself to move freely in your rehearsal space. Concentrate on taking risks with what you do and say and responding boldly with your whole body according to your impulses. Your body should feel alive and dynamic, like all of you is pursuing the Action.

Now you are ready to act your staging.

Acting Your Staging

- Do a Countdown. On the GO, begin your monologue, and now *use* all of your lines and staging to pursue your Action. Continue to the end of the monologue, no matter what.

- With your partner, compare the differences you saw between doing just the staging and fully *acting* the staging. Doing just the staging should look fairly mechanical. Acting the staging with the Action should look real, alive, and expressive.

- Your acting should be as truthful and connected in the staging as it is in any of the other exercises. If you think it wasn't, you can work on it by going back to the As-If when you lose the connection to the Action. Once you have it again, continue with the staging and the lines.

Act your staging several times without judging the results. Watch your partner work and notice what you see. Is he as connected to the Action in the lines and staging as he is in his As-If? Is he *using* his staging to communicate his Action? Look for the following qualities in your own and in your partner's work:

- *Discover and act on the first moment fully.* Use the Countdown to challenge yourself to play the first moment without preplanning it. Trust all of the work you have put into your staging and let that first moment be anything. It can even be "I don't know what to do now," or "I forgot my Action." Express *that* with the line and the staging. Stay in, which leads to another truthful moment as you reconnect to the Action. Staying in helps you act immediately—to think on your feet—instead of waiting until you feel like it. It helps you learn to trust yourself on stage.

- *Support your voice.* Speak up right away, and act fully with your voice in the first moment and throughout the monologue. Stop waiting until you're sure; you may never be!

- *Stay in physically.* Keep your body engaged and in the moment. You can think of yourself as "leading with your body." If you notice yourself flopping your hands down to your sides between Chunks, go back and practice making your transitions active. You should experience yourself as constantly in motion (even when you are standing in one place) throughout the entire monologue. Engaging your body helps you "take out the stops" (below).

- *Stay consistent with your focus point.* If your monologue is addressed to one other character, make sure you keep coming back to the same point, so it doesn't look like the other character is moving around as you move. For this and for other kinds of focus, have your partner watch and tell you if you are consistent.

- *Constantly reconnect to the cap of the Action.* In chapter 5 I discussed keeping the cap, or goal, of your Action in mind as you act. Make sure you are still checking in with the cap at this stage. If you get lost, simply stay in, and ask yourself, "Is she 'giving me a commitment' now?" Act on the information you receive.

- *Let everything be in.* Especially at this stage, when you are working to integrate everything, accept and play anything that happens, including awkward moments or rough transitions. Practice making everything part of the Story of your monologue *this time.* Doing so keeps you from "commenting" on your monologue as you play it, as if to say *"This* belongs in the monologue but *this* doesn't" as you work. Watch a partner work on letting everything be in and notice how the rough spots almost always fit right into the Story.

- *Let the monologue affect you.* All of the techniques in this book are designed so that you have something specific to do, whether you feel connected to your monologue at an audition or not, so that you can act under pressure. But never forget why you like the monologue, and always be willing for the words to affect you.

- *Keep the staging specific.* Take note of whether you are losing your Sizes and Speeds, or your commitment to your movements and gestures. If you are, go back and drill your staging.

- *Allow no "stops" and no "flops."* Notice if your monologue tends to stop and start, which most often happens when your transitions between Chunks are unclear. Also notice if you are flopping your arms down at the end of a Chunk. Keep them engaged. Flopping says "not really" or "I give up." A stop or a flop could also be a place where you're in the habit of pausing to remember the line or a part of the staging. If you flop or stop, work on your lines and staging until your monologue has a complete flow from beginning to end.

- *Let it go.* Your monologue is only two minutes long! Sometimes actors want to "hold on" to the monologue in an attempt to control the moments, but holding on only slows them down and keeps them out of the moment. Practice letting your monologue mean whatever it means this time. Address any problems in the "Troubleshooting" section (below).

The "Long Run" of your Monologue

Each quality listed in the previous section should happen every time you perform your monologue. In the beginning, you'll have to keep devoting energy and concentration to all of them. After a while though, they'll become habitual and you will be left with simply playing the moments of your monologue each time you perform it.

As you work further, you may notice sometimes that the As-If is falling away and that your attention is simply on the task at hand, the Action. That is perfectly natural and, in fact, is the whole purpose of the As-If. The As-If is there to explain the Action to you and your body: "This is what 'to lay down the law' is like to me." Once your body has learned that explanation, it becomes less important to think about the As-If while you pursue the Action with the lines and staging of the monologue. Your body now associates that Action with that monologue, and you are free to perform it.

This process is especially the case when this technique is used in scenes. After the As-If has been used by an actor to explain the Action to himself in rehearsal, he is then free to focus completely on the other actors on stage in performance. In monologues, though, you don't have another person in front of you to work with. Therefore, it may help you to keep the As-If with you longer so you have something specific to focus on. Or, you may have no problem simply focusing on the Action after the As-If has done its job. You are also free to come up with new As-Ifs for the same Action if the one you're using gets stale. These options I leave up to you and to whatever you find works best in a particular monologue.

You may also notice that working with the Action naturally "smoothes out" the more mechanical and stagy aspects of your movement and gesture. This smoothing is exactly what is supposed to happen. Both your Action and your staging are the ways you've chosen to express your interpretation of your monologue. They come from the same source—you—and with practice they will come together to express your Story.

Troubleshooting

Here are seven common questions and problems that might come up when you combine the acting with the staging, and ways to address them.

1. I'm having trouble connecting with my Action when I do my monologue because there are so many different moves in my staging that I'm focusing only on remembering them all.

• You may have broken down your monologue into too many Chunks, or you may have used too much movement to express the Chunks you have. Go back and see if there are some Chunks you can combine into longer ones. Also try simplifying your movements. You should be able to memorize all your moves fairly easily.

2. I'm fine when I'm doing the Action and the As-If; but when I do the staging, I find myself making the same types of gestures over and over during the Chunks. I don't feel like the staging is specific enough.

• You may have too few Chunks in your monologue. If you have fewer than seven for a two-minute monologue, try breaking it down further. A couple more Chunks will make you more specific when you write the additional Descriptions and create staging for them.

3. Several places in my monologue feel really fake and indicated.

• Identify whether the indication is in the acting or in the staging. Work without the staging, allowing yourself to move freely, as you pursue your Action with the lines. Does it still feel fake or indicated? If not, it's in the staging.

• Identify the places in the staging that feel too big to you and bring them down a little. If you're clenching both fists, clench one, for example. Then perform your adjusted staging fully with your Action.

• Try the videotaping suggestion in problem 4, below.

4. My partner says I can "go farther" with what I'm doing in my monologue, but I'm afraid of overacting.

• Try increasing your commitment to the Action and the specificity in your staging, and have your partner tell you if and when you are overacting. Overacting usually happens when an actor does something unconnected or general with a huge amount of energy. If you are truly connected with the Action in the moment, and if you are specific with your use of the staging, you won't overact.

• Try videotaping yourself doing the monologue as it is now (but don't look at it yet). Then try one or more of the following:

- Make the stakes in your As-If more important, and rehearse it with a partner. Then act the monologue with all of your staging, and videotape that version.

- Now look at the two versions (watch them many times so that you get over the self-consciousness of seeing yourself). What, if anything, looks overacted to you?. Often what feels huge to us is not huge at all on the stage. Every actor has to find his own point of comparison between what something feels like internally and what it actually looks like.

5. There are several places in my monologue where I have a feeling of being vague and of not knowing what I'm doing.

- Identify whether the vagueness is in the acting or in the staging. Try going through your staging without acting several times, to see if you can consistently perform *every detail* of your movements, gestures, and Sizes and Speeds. If you can, then the vagueness is in the acting.

- Make sure you know why you have chosen that particular Action, and make sure you know exactly what you want in your As-If and why it is important to you. Also make sure you are boldly taking risks in the moment.

6. I'm doing an aggressive monologue where the character is telling off his brother, and I feel like I'm yelling the whole time.

- Apply the following advice to any one-note monologue:

- Check the words of your Descriptions and make sure you have variety in your staging choices. If you need more variety, change some of them.

- Make sure you have an As-If important enough to you that you would willingly use different approaches in the moment to achieve the Action. Then, with a partner, deliberately try a bunch of different ways of pursuing your Action in the moment, such as "joking," "teasing," "inspiring," "demanding," "pleading," and "threatening," to loosen up these sides of yourself. Make sure also that you are not just "telling off" the person in your As-If but that you are trying to get him to do something you really need.

7. I'm sick of this monologue and I don't want to do it anymore!

- Rehearse and audition with it anyway. Some of your best work will happen when you don't feel like performing a piece, especially when you know it well. This situation is one you hope will arise in your career—as in a long-running show. You now have the opportunity to work on keeping your monologue fresh, as a professional.

- Challenge yourself by preparing a whole new monologue.

Adjusting the Size of Your Monologue

There are a number of ways you can very easily take your monologue down in size while keeping the specificity in your staging. These methods make it possible for you to use the same monologue for a theater or a film audition, or to simplify a monologue with a great deal of movement if you are directed to do so.

If you have a monologue with a lot of movement, try performing it standing in one place, keeping the Sizes and Speeds, the transitions, and the gestures. Try only moving one step forward at the climax.

To perform the monologue in a chair, simply make the seat of the chair into your square! Use the potential movement you have in a chair to express your staging; keep your Sizes and Speeds; and use your gestures, adjusting their size as well. Practice it until the overall size of the staging feels right in the chair.

As you practice, make sure you keep the intensity of your commitment to your Action and your commitment to your Sizes and Speeds present in your performance. Watch others perform these adjustments. Notice that, when an actor stays specific and engaged, the size of her performance does not interfere with its intensity.

If you have followed all of the steps so far, you are well on your way to a rewarding actor-director collaboration with yourself. Investing this much care and consideration in the directing and the acting of your monologue should be paying off with a dynamic, fun-to-perform audition monologue.

I encourage you to work on new monologues as soon as possible. When you do, I think you'll be surprised to find how much more quickly the work goes. Have fun with the challenges of a new monologue, and use all of the steps to make it an enjoyable way to express yourself as an actor and as a director. The rest of the book is about introducing yourself in the audition room, auditioning, and ways to improve all of your audition experiences.

Checklist for Acting Your Staging

❑ You are discovering and acting the first moment fully after the Countdown.

❑ You are pursuing your Action throughout your monologue, no matter what, without stopping.

❑ You are using your voice fully.

❑ Your staging, especially your Sizes and Speeds, is intact.

❑ There are no stops, and no flops—you're staying in during the whole monologue.

❑ Your focus choice is clear and consistent throughout the monologue.

❑ You are reconnecting with your cap throughout the monologue.

❑ You are playing the truth of the moment no matter what it is.

❑ You are sustaining your last moment, continuing to play your Action.

❑ You have identified any problems in your Acting or Staging, and addressed them using solutions from the Troubleshooting section, or have come up with your own.

❑ You have experimented with adjusting the overall size of your monologue.

PART 3
Auditioning with Your Monologue

CHAPTER 8

ENTRANCES AND EXITS

When you audition, you do many things other than perform your monologues. A typical audition includes greeting the auditors; introducing yourself and your monologues; transitioning between monologues; interacting with the auditors; and leaving the room.

For many actors, these nonperforming moments are the most nerve-wracking parts of an audition. The way you handle them can work in your favor or detract from the overall effect of your audition. In this chapter, I discuss each element completely so that you can take advantage of the many opportunities you have to communicate positive things about yourself as a performer when you audition.

The key to making your nonperforming moments work for you is to put yourself in the shoes of a director who is looking for actors. An actor who enters, auditions, and leaves with a sense of confidence and enjoyment, no matter how well or how badly he thinks he has done, shows something important to a director. Even if he obviously made a mistake in his monologue, he still finishes strongly, with a self-assured "thank you" and exit from the room. He doesn't try to get an indication from the director as to whether she liked his audition or not. He leaves confidently and goes about his business. In that situation, the director might think, "There's an actor who can keep going even if something goes wrong, and the last part of his audition was strong. I'll ask him to come back."

On the other hand, an actor might give a strong audition, but then "apologize for herself" at the end. She'll say "thank you" as if to say, "I'm sorry, it has really gone much better before." In this case, the director might think, "Well, maybe that *wasn't* so great. If the actor thinks it was terrible, then maybe it was— she knows her monologue much better than I do."

These situations happen every day. In both of them, the actors "told" the director how they expected her to regard their auditions, and the director did exactly as the actors asked. What do you "tell" the people who audition you to think of your work?

It's easy to fall into the trap of communicating "Please cast me; I want this so much!" when you audition. Or "Please cast me; I haven't had an acting job in a year." Or "Please cast me, I've never had an acting job and I want you to validate me as an actor." I think you'll agree that the only thing really being communicated is desperation. Sometimes actors try to use the reverse psychology of "I don't need you, you need me." Out of insecurity, they come in with an arrogant attitude that is supposed to communicate confidence.

If you were a director or casting director or agent, would you want to work with desperate or arrogant actors? What kind of actors would you want to work with? As a director, I want to work with actors who treat themselves as professionals, which includes being

- Well trained

- Prepared

- Energetic

- Mature (at any age)

- Ready to take chances and to collaborate fully

- Good ensemble players, even (especially) if they're the stars

- Respectful (to themselves and to everyone involved in a show)

- Excited about the project

- Reliable

- Committed 100 percent to the work

- Enjoyable to work with

Chances are, you have read other books about auditioning or have already done a lot of this thinking on your own. The question is, How can you communicate these things about yourself in an audition? Some of them show in your monologue. It is obvious when you're prepared and committed to your performance. Others are communicated with your attitude in the rest of the audition.

I think an actor would want to know for sure that she consistently presents herself and her work in a positive light in auditions. I suggest the most effective way to do this is by *acting* the non-acting parts of the audition. By "acting" I *don't* suggest you be phony or pretend you're another person. Instead, use fun, positive Actions in order to communicate the best parts of yourself as an actor to your auditors.

Positive Entrances and Exits

When we work on entrances and exits in class, I first ask the actors to play around with the *worst* ways of introducing themselves, using Actions that engender some of the self-sabotaging behaviors I described in the previous section. I have them say, "Hello, my name is _____, and I will be doing a monologue from _____," with the following Actions:

- To beg forgiveness

- To put a jerk in his place

- To kiss ass (not an actual action, but a common attitude)

I then ask them to say "thank you" and leave, playing the same Action on the way out. The results are usually met with howls of laughter and recognition. I ask the class what they think actors with these attitudes would be like to work with in a show.

All three of these attitudes are common in the audition room. Sometimes they come from actors who are very good at what they do. They may actually be trying to communicate positive things about themselves but aren't yet aware of how their attitudes actually come across in auditions.

The beg-forgiveness actor may be such a perfectionist about her work (which can be a great quality to work with) that she unknowingly shows the director her ruthless "critique" of herself the moment she finishes performing. All the director might see, however, is an actor who forever needs constant hand-holding and reinforcement during rehearsals and shows—an energy drain.

The put-you-in-your-place actor may be working hard—too hard—on appearing confident in auditions. All an experienced director will be able to imagine, however, is what it will be like to give this actor notes the night before performances start!

The kiss-your-ass actor may be trying too hard to show the director he is enthusiastic and willing to do anything the director needs of him. Unfortunately, this attitude can make it seem as if the actor is only interested in advancing himself. Directors know that actors who really do have this attitude can destroy the unity in a cast with their constant attempts to win favor.

The moments before and after your monologue are the only opportunity the people who audition you have to get a sense of what you're like to work with. Therefore, it is a crucial time for you and for them. The good news is: If a certain Action can make an actor come across in an apologetic or obnoxious or phony way, another Action can make her come across in a professionally desirable way.

Positive Actions

Here are several Actions that communicate positive things about you as a performer:

- If you want to communicate that you are a thoroughly reliable and prepared actor, you might use the Action *"to convince a friend to put himself completely in my hands,"* or "to *convince a friend to accept my guarantee."*

- If you want to communicate that you are genuinely enthusiastic about the project that is being cast, and that you'd love to work on it, you might use the Action *"to convince a friend to join forces with me."*

Don't make your Action about getting the job, such as "to get a fair chance" or "to get a commitment." Getting the job is not in your control. Making a positive statement about the kind of performer you are *is* in your control.

Positive As-Ifs

As-Ifs for entrance and exit Actions should always be about completely positive, fun things that you feel good about doing. To find them, call on the generous, confident, and loving parts of yourself: It's as if you're assuring your dearest friend that you will take care of an important task for her wedding, for example; or it's as if you're convincing your friend to go with you on the vacation you've both been dreaming of.

Big and Slow

Looking back over past auditions, job interviews, or any other situation in which you were under pressure, what was your most usual Size and Speed? It's easy to get Small and Fast when nervous or Small and Slow when unsure. Big and Fast can be fun, but it can overwhelm your auditors. I suggest using Big and Slow for all the non-monologue parts of your audition because it comes across as the most confident, poised and relaxed Size and Speed.

With a partner, try introducing yourselves using each Size and Speed. Notice how Big and Slow feels and looks compared to the others. I think you'll find as an actor that it calms you down, and that it gives an auditor the chance to settle in and really take in an actor before he auditions.

Introducing Yourself

Now think about exactly what you will say when you introduce yourself and your pieces. In some cases you will know the people who audition you, and they will greet you by name when you come in the door. If not, have a way to state your name clearly, and to say which monologues you're doing, that uses the same words every time.

It's easy to stumble in an introduction so you'll want to memorize it just like you've memorized your monologue. Decide whether you need to include the name of the playwright (for well-known plays, it's not necessary). Decide whether you need to name the character.

Very important: "voice" a period at the end of each of your sentences, not a question mark. "Hello, I'm _____. This is Yelena's monologue from Uncle Vanya." Do not say, "Hello, my name is _____? This is Yelena's monologue from Uncle Vanya?"

Practicing Your Introduction

To practice a positive introduction, begin by speaking your positive As-If directly to a partner, staying Big and Slow. When you feel you are performing the As-If fully, introduce yourself and your monologue, while continuing both to play your positive Action and to stay Big and Slow. Have your partner give you feedback on whether you were as positive, and as Big and Slow, in the introduction as you were in your As-If.

It's natural to become self-conscious at first when practicing your introduction. Practice until you get over any self-consciousness, and until you can introduce yourself with confidence and poise every time.

Rehearsing Your Entrance

There are several more details to consider in the moments leading up to the start of your monologue. Paying conscious attention to each of them gives you a confident, assured entrance to any audition.

It is extremely helpful to practice each of the following points with a partner. In class, I ask the actors to demonstrate both the "right" and the "wrong" way of doing each point. The actors are usually amazed to discover the effects that each way has on potential auditors. As you walk in the door, Big and Slow:

- *Make eye contact with the auditors.* If they don't look at you at first because they are talking to each other or writing, continue with the following. Be ready, however, to make eye contact with them at any time.

- *Place the square.* As I discussed in chapter 3, make sure your square is behind the point in the audition room that is too close to the auditors. Practice so that you are able to place the square easily, without looking down to the floor.

- *Note your focus point.* After you place your square, notice where in the room you will focus your monologue.

- *Move to the place in the square from which you will introduce yourself.* Introduce yourself from either the Centerstage part of your square or the Upstage Center. If your monologue starts in one of those places, stay there. If it starts from the Upstage Right or Left corners or from any other place in the square, simply turn and walk there, keeping your head up, when you've finished your introduction. Introducing yourself from one of the Upstage corners would feel "off balance."

- *Take your cues from the auditors.* Don't chat, shake hands, or approach them unless they initiate it. Unless this happens, go directly to the place you have chosen to introduce yourself. Approaching them to shake hands, especially if they're not quite ready, can make them feel invaded. If you need to give them your picture before you introduce yourself, do it simply, staying Big and Slow.

- *Don't speak until you've arrived at your introduction spot and have stopped moving.* Saying hello and introducing yourself the minute you open the door can be jarring to you and to them. Instead, play your positive Action silently until you've arrived at your introduction spot. Doing this gives them a chance to take you in or finish up their notes from the last audition, and it gives you a moment to orient yourself in the room.

- *Remember to breathe!* As you practice your entrance, also make a habit of remembering places to check in with your breathing. For example, when you open the door, on your way to your introduction spot, and in your Countdown, check your breathing. Breathing helps your nerves and reminds you to support your voice.

Now practice your entire entrance.

- Walk in the door, Big and Slow, playing your positive Action silently.

- Make eye contact with the auditors if they are looking at you. Unless they initiate conversation, proceed.

- If they have your picture, continue with the following. If you need to give it to them, do so, remaining Big and Slow.

- As you walk to your introduction spot, subtly place your square and notice your focus point.

- When you have completely stopped, and have made eye contact with the auditors, introduce yourself and your monologue to them with your positive Action, Big and Slow.

- Start your Countdown.

- On GO, begin acting your monologue.

As you can see, there is a great deal to practice for your entrance! Doing so faithfully with a partner, until all of the above points are habitual, makes your entrance confident and professional, and frees you to deal assuredly with the different audition environments you will encounter.

Introducing Two Monologues

Adjust your introduction: "Hi, I'm _____, and today I'll be doing a monologue from _____ and one from _____." Introducing both of your monologues in the beginning makes it easier on you and makes the whole audition smoother. You won't be coming back "as yourself" in the middle to introduce the second piece.

Transitioning Between Monologues

Transitioning cleanly between contrasting monologues can look very impressive:

- At the end of the first monologue, hold the moment, sustaining your Action.

- Moving Big and Slow, come out of the staging without looking down at the floor or at the auditors.

- Go to the starting place for your second monologue, and begin the next Countdown.

- Start your next monologue.

It's important to practice the transition Big and Slow, so that your auditors will know for sure that you are ending the first monologue and starting the next one.

What Should I Wear?

Because dressing inappropriately can detract from even a strong performance, here are some pointers for general monologue auditions:

- Dress neatly and show self-esteem.

- If you are doing one monologue, wear clothes that subtly suggest the character—you don't have to costume yourself completely.

- If you are doing two contrasting monologues, dress neutrally and let your choices in the monologues bring out the differences in the characters.

- Wear comfortable clothes and stable shoes that you can easily move around in.

- Avoid distractions like flip-flops, platform shoes that make you walk funny, lots of noisy jewelry, or too much makeup.

- Never wear your hair in a way that allows it to fall in your face while you are acting. If you have long hair, pull it back so they can clearly see your face.

- Look as much like your picture as possible.

Rehearsing Your Exit

At the end of a monologue, remember to hold the last moment, still playing the Action, so that you don't drop or pop out of it suddenly. This practice gives you a moment to become Big and Slow, and to switch to your positive exit Action. It gives the auditors time to adjust their focus too. Then:

- Staying Big and Slow, bring your attention down from your Focus point to make eye contact with the auditors. Don't look down at the floor in between. This gentle transition looks very confident and focused.

- Playing your positive Action, say a simple "thank you," and begin to leave the room, staying Big and Slow. If they want to talk to you about the piece or anything else, fine, but let it come from them. If not, keep your head up (it can be tempting to duck your head) and exit, staying Big and Slow.

Like the entrance, a confident exit requires practice with a partner. It can be tempting to "get the audition over with" by dropping out of your monologue as soon as it ends and rushing from the room. Don't ruin your carefully rehearsed audition by doing so! Show esteem for yourself and for your work by rehearsing your exit until you can consistently sustain the last moment of your monologue, and stay Big and Slow as you say "thank you" and leave playing your positive Action.

The End of the Audition

I suggest you always expect to leave after you perform your monologue(s) unless the auditors start a conversation with you. Leaving shows them that you are respectful of their time, and keeps you from looking for their reactions to your audition.

Many actors try to engage the auditors in conversation before and after they audition. Unfortunately, it often works against them. Directors and casting directors frequently have a lot at stake and have many decisions to make in a short period of time. Dealing with the hellos and goodbyes of the auditions is just as difficult for them—and they have to do it all day. Respect their situation by letting them initiate any extra conversation. If they don't have time to chat, they will be grateful to you, and it will make you appear considerate, confident, and professional.

If the auditors do want to talk to you before or after the audition, think about what you might say, and how you can say it succinctly. Often they'll ask you to tell them what you've been up to lately, or to tell them a little about yourself. Sometimes auditors do this so that they can see what you're like apart from your monologue. I suggest you prepare simple, concise things to say about yourself if you are asked these questions. If you're not prepared, you may not know what to say to present yourself in the most positive light, or you may forget something they should know.

Make a list of a few short sentences that describe what you've been doing. Tell them where you grew up, where you've gone to school, and how long you've lived in the city you're auditioning in. Tell them about the last project you acted in. If you haven't worked much yet, tell them about any classes you've taken; let them know you're auditioning for everything you can. If you are currently in a show, tell them about it—briefly—and say you'll send them an invitation. Be honest and demonstrate self-esteem about your activities, even if all you've done so far is take classes. Decide what you will tell them, and practice saying it with your positive Action.

Checklist for Entrances and Exits

❑ You have chosen a positive Action and As-If for your entrance and exit, and you have practiced the Action with your introduction and thank you, Big and Slow.

❑ You have practiced all the details of your entrance, playing your positive Action.

❑ You have practiced introducing and transitioning between two monologues.

❑ You have noted how you might dress appropriately for auditions with one or more monologues.

❑ You have practiced all the details of your exit, playing your positive Action.

❑ You know what you will say if auditors ask you about yourself.

CHAPTER 9

THE AUDITION

If you have completed all of the work in this book so far, you now have an entire audition prepared. In this chapter, I show you a powerful tool for giving yourself productive feedback *after* you audition, as well as fun and challenging ways to practice auditioning with other actors. I also discuss taking direction in auditions.

Auditions are agony for some actors. Other actors enjoy the audition process. If auditioning is at all unpleasant for you, you're not alone. When an interviewer asked William H. Macy to name the best thing about being nominated for an Academy Award, Macy said, "The best thing is, I don't have to audition anymore."

Often an actor's anxiety about auditioning comes not from how auditors treat him, but from how he treats himself afterward. Does this sound familiar to you? Many actors are their own worst enemy after an audition. They can pick an audition apart for hours, days, even weeks.

This next section is intended especially for you if you have experienced any sort of anguish after you've auditioned. And if you're able to handle auditioning without completely going out of your mind, this section is still extremely helpful, because it gives you a way to improve your auditions for as long as you do them. Following is a way of talking to yourself that is useful in your whole career—not just for auditions but for your rehearsals and performances too.

Giving Yourself Feedback

Let's go to the moment right after you've left the audition room. Anticipating and preparing the audition, and then finally doing it, have generated a huge amount of energy. Now is the moment when the audition is freshest in your mind, and when you can use that energy most productively.

As soon as possible (and I suggest you always schedule extra time before you have to be somewhere else so you can do this), sit down in a quiet place where you can be alone, and answer the following five questions. The answers to these questions should only be about factors that are in your control. If your auditors laughed hysterically during your comedic monologue, or if they said you did a wonderful job, great. Let yourself enjoy it. But their reactions are never in your control, so don't write them down.

1. What Worked? What are some factors in your control that could have worked well in an audition? Here are only a few examples. When you make this list after an audition, write down every little thing that worked—even that you liked what you wore to the audition.

- My voice was strong and connected.
- My staging was completely memorized.
- I stayed Big & Slow during my exit.

2. Why did it work? What things did you do to make the above factors work? Writing them down will remind you to repeat them in the future.

- I work on my voice regularly. I warmed up this morning.
- I drilled my staging until it was memorized. I practiced it regularly leading up to this audition.
- I practiced my exits with my friend until I was always Big and Slow.

3. What could have worked better? This question is *not,* "What did I do wrong?" "What went horribly?" Or even, "What didn't work?". Speak to yourself as positively as possible. Remember to write down only the factors that are in your control.

- I was late.
- I did not pursue my Action fully.

• I stumbled on the words of my introduction.

4. Why could it have worked better? How did you not take control of these factors as much as you could have? What did you leave up to chance?

• I didn't plan enough time to get to the audition.

• I have not practiced acting this monologue with a partner for two months.

• I have never decided and rehearsed how to introduce this monologue.

5. What am I going to do for the next audition? Now make a list that reminds you to repeat your work on the factors that did work, and to fix the factors that could have worked better.

• I'm going to continue to work on my voice. I'm going to warm up before every audition.

• I'm going to drill my staging regularly, leading up to the audition.

• I'm going to continue to practice staying Big and Slow in my exits.

• I'm going to plan so I can get to the audition early.

• I'm going to practice the Action of this monologue regularly with a friend.

• I'm going to decide and rehearse exactly how I'm going to introduce this monologue.

The list for your answer to question 5 is the most important part of your feedback. It's a list of *exactly* what you need to keep remembering to do, and what you need to work on. It is the key to improving your next audition, and is a positive challenge: "I *know* I can repeat the things that worked and fix the others!" It is important to list the factors that did work, and why they worked, because it's easy to take them for granted. If you don't write them down you're likely to forget that they worked because you did something specific about them. It is crucial that you *write* your answers to all five questions. Giving yourself feedback mentally is not enough.

This process is about taking the "drama" out of auditioning. Sometimes, "because show business is so fickle *anyway,*" we leave too much up to chance. We put the drama into "Will I get there in time?" "Will I feel connected to a monologue I haven't practiced in three weeks?" "Will I magically be exactly what they are looking for, regardless of how I audition?" Instead, keep the drama *in the monologue.* Misplaced drama often plagues shows: everyone is tempted to put the drama into not being prepared, into politics, or into whether the set will come in at budget instead of into the play itself.

This method of feedback has changed my life as a director. During rehearsals and performances, I use it to affirm what is working and to note what I would do differently next time. I apply it to my own preparation; working with actors, designers, producers, and stage managers; and to the overall quality of the working atmosphere. When something could be working better, I find it incredibly comforting to write it down so I know that, no matter what, I can learn from any experience.

The final part of this process is to develop the habit of not allowing yourself to think about how an audition went after you have completed the questions. If you do find yourself obsessing about an audition, do one or both of the following:

• Take out your response to question #5 and take immediate action on a factor that is in your control (schedule a practice session; find a good voice teacher).

• Examine your In My Control-Not In My Control list. Identify whether what you're worrying about is or isn't in your control. If it is in your control, take action. If it isn't, choose something on the list that is and take action on that (go to the bookstore or library and find a great new monologue; go over your auditioning wardrobe; look through recent audition listings).

Don't underestimate the power of this tool. Do you see that, if you answer the questions after *every* audition and take action based on your answers, your auditions can't help but improve? Do it consistently, even if it seems obvious or repetitive to write down every little thing.

The five feedback questions can also work wonderfully for your rehearsals and performances in productions. If you take a moment at the end of the day to answer the questions, you can leave your performance at the theater, instead of worrying about it for the rest of the night.

Treating your work as professionally and as encouragingly as possible calms you down and frees up energy to truly improve your auditioning and performing experiences. A great way to use this system is to have a special notebook in which you ask yourself the five questions and keep the responses all in one place. Looking back over them will give you satisfaction because you will be able to track your progress.

Audition Exercises

In the last class of my monologue workshop, the actors audition each other in three different environments, each of which is designed to test the actors' focus in a different way. I describe these exercises here so you can try them with your friends. The more people you can get together the more you will get out of the exercises and the more fun you will have. (I suggest six to eight people.)

Divide into two groups: the Casting People and the Actors. Switch functions after each type of audition environment. Everyone should agree that while the Casting People's behavior will often challenge the Actors, none of these environments is meant to be mean-spirited.

Casting People: Organize yourselves by deciding who will call the actors into the room, who will talk to them, and who will simply watch or perform the other activities I describe below.

Actors: Pretend you are at an actual audition: Wait until you are called; go in and perform your entire audition; and then write down your feedback as soon as you are finished. Take advantage of the fact that this is only an exercise by observing your reactions to each environment.

The Neutral Audition

In the Neutral audition, the Casting People are to be as expressionless as possible (i.e., no laughing or other responses during the monologues). One of the Casting People should call the Actors into the room. When the Actor comes in, all Casting

People should just stare straight at her during her audition. One Casting Person should give a straight, simple "thank you" at the end. No one should smile at the actor. When all the actors have auditioned, switch places.

The Chaos Audition

The Chaos audition tests the Actors' concentration and their ability to refocus during the distracting things that happen at many auditions. The job of the Casting People is to create a high energy, distracting environment during the audition. One Casting Person should act as the head casting director, or the director of "the project" that the audition is for. Someone else should keep time so that the audition only goes on for four minutes (the timekeeper should strictly enforce the time limit). The Casting People can repeatedly redirect the actor; ask the actor to try the monologue in different styles and accents; bicker among themselves; talk on the phone; and perform any other distracting activity they can think of. The Actors should revenge themselves fully when they become the Casting People.

The Positive Audition

In the Positive audition, the Casting People create an "ideal" auditioning environment. They should be friendly, relaxed, and appreciative. They should laugh in appropriate places and give glowing comments afterward. They should chat with the actor after the audition, giving him a chance to practice the suggestions in chapter 8. When all of the actors have auditioned, switch places.

After the Audition Exercises

What were your reactions as an Actor? It's interesting to notice which environment was most comfortable and which was most uncomfortable. Some actors hate the Neutral audition. Because of the lack of response, they find themselves pushing and redirecting their monologue. Did you fall into that trap? Some actors are most comfortable in the Chaos audition. Accepting how out of control and self-involved the Casting People are actually relaxes them and helps them stay in the moment. Some actors find the Positive audition unnerving because there's no way of knowing if the comments are sincere.

Were you able to make your feedback after each audition constructive? How was your concentration in each environment? What threw off your concentration? The point is not to avoid being thrown off—who wouldn't be in a situation like the Chaos audition? The exercises give you opportunities to practice refocusing *when you are* thrown off in auditions.

My friend Paul walked out of the Chaos audition exercise. He saw no reason to tolerate such behavior. I challenged him on this point by asking what he had to gain by leaving. Could he imagine keeping his composure while pursuing his intentions for his monologue, even if his work was not even noticed by the self-involved Casting People? Shortly after this, he went to an audition for an agent who asked him for a monologue. While he was performing it the agent talked on the phone and rummaged for papers in her desk, seeming to pay no attention. Inwardly, he assumed she hated what he was doing, but decided to recommit to his Action and finish the monologue for himself. After he finished, he was surprised when she said, "Yeah, we'll send you out. Put our number on your résumé and keep in touch."

In no way do I approve of the behavior of the agent in this story, which was rude and disrespectful. She probably saw that Paul was prepared and specific, knew she wanted to work with him, and went about her business without thinking of how her behavior might affect him. Certainly there are some professional situations you should not tolerate, and only you can decide what they are. But I suggest you have nothing to gain by trying to change them, and you may have a lot to gain by letting much of other people's unprofessional behavior roll off your back, because it's everywhere in this business. Concentrate instead on what *you* want to do, and audition for your own satisfaction.

These audition exercises can help exorcise your worst fears of, or actual experiences with, auditions by allowing you to deliberately create them and meet them head-on in a supportive environment. Many actors in my class leave with an empowering sense of being able to get through any kind of audition after these exercises.

What did you learn as a Casting Person? Many actors who do this exercise are surprised at what they see from the other side of the table. As Casting People they notice how quickly they get a sense of what an actor is like, and how prepared and invested he is in his monologue. They also get a sense of what it must be like to see audition after audition, all day long, and why most auditors' responses to actors are not personal. They just have a tremendous amount of work to do.

The overall lesson from these exercises is *never* to take your auditors' responses, or lack of them, personally. Stick to your own goals. If you do happen to get some advice you feel is valuable at an audition, take it. For the rest of the time, you can learn not to abandon yourself to the whims and reactions of others, and to keep your own counsel about how well you do in auditions. When you practice this attitude, over time it makes you more self-reliant and more secure in your own work because you don't buy into the drama of "what they said."

Taking Direction

What if you were directed to change things about your thoroughly prepared monologue in an audition? Practicing for this eventuality can be fun and can build your confidence about taking direction in auditions and rehearsals. It can be done as a separate practice session or as part of the audition exercises.

I've already discussed how to adjust the overall size of your monologue (see chapter 7). I think you'll find that, because you've put so much specific work into your monologue, it costs you little to change the overall interpretation, if asked. The ways you can put immediate changes into it are

• Change the staging

• Change the As-If

• Change the Action

First, try changing your Sizes and Speeds in response to direction. You've already experienced how Size and Speed choices can dramatically affect the impact of a monologue, and you can make such changes instantly. If you are given an emotional direction, like "sadder" or "more excited," try adjusting some of your Sizes and Speeds to Small and Slow or Big and Fast, respectively. Try it for yourself, just on a physical level, and see how it works for you.

If you are given a direction about the stakes of the monologue; for example, that it should be "more important" or "lighter," try changing the As-If to one that has higher stakes or is more fun.

If you are asked to change the overall interpretation of your monologue, change the Action. If the director says, "I think he is desperate in this monologue," pick an Action that helps communicate that quality, such as "to beg for another chance." If the director thinks the character should be aggressive, try an Action such as "smack someone into reality".

Practice giving and taking direction with other actors. I think you will be surprised at how easy it can be to adjust quickly for a desired result. Specificity breeds specificity, and if you are already specific in your acting and your directing, you can change to another choice quickly and with commitment.

Always take it as a positive sign if you are directed in a monologue audition. You may be directed because the director saw in your performance that you work specifically, and he now wants to see how easily you take direction. If your performance had been vague and uncommitted, he may not even have bothered!

If you have been successfully doing all of the work up until this point, congratulations! I hope you are looking forward to challenging yourself and enjoying your work on monologues and auditions more than ever before.

Checklist for the Audition

❑ You and your partners have auditioned each other in the Neutral, Chaotic, and Positive environments.

❑ You gave yourself feedback after each audition environment, including your entrance, monologue performance, and exit.

❑ You practiced taking direction.

Afterword: A Positive and Habitual Approach to Auditioning and Working

When you regularly practice a positive approach to your auditions, as in the feedback exercise in chapter 9, you make your work attractive and challenging. Each audition or role becomes an experience you can learn and benefit from. If, however, you start every search for a new monologue with an internal debate about whether you really want to be an actor, you're sabotaging yourself by making your work unpleasant.

When you make something a habit, you need to devote less energy to doing it. Weeding out any unproductive habits you have incorporated into your preparation for auditions frees up energy to create positive, productive ones. I suggest you commit, for a time, to habitualizing the following positive conditions and practices in your life as an auditioning actor; then agree to reevaluate your satisfaction at the end of that time, *not* while you are establishing them.

- Make the most of what your life as an actor is right now. Establish an efficient and enjoyable routine for finding material you like, preparing monologues, submitting yourself for auditions, and making artistic and business contacts. By making these efforts habitual, you are taking the pressure off of individual auditions, and days when you feel like you are not getting anywhere.

- Make your business practices simple and professional.

- Define the kind of actor you would want to work with if you were a director, and work to become that actor.

- Take charge of your training and decide which skills are most important for you to work on.

- Have an acting approach that is reliable and makes sense to you.

- Do everything in your control to make yourself more hirable and your work more satisfying: prepare a variety of monologues; work regularly on your voice, speech and body; develop new skills; and go on as many auditions as possible.

- Think of each audition in the long term. Each audition is not just for a single role but for as long as you and the people you audition for remain in the business. Therefore, if you don't get cast, you can still get satisfaction from giving a strong audition that will likely be remembered for the next project.

- See and read as much work as possible so that you can identify the people with whom you would most like to work.

- Build supportive working relationships with other actors.

- Make the most of every project you work on.

- Accept that any comments about your work, bad *or* good, are completely out of your control.

- Refuse to talk to yourself negatively about your work, and never apologize for your work to anyone.

- Evaluate your work positively so you can benefit from every experience you have.

- Work and audition for *your own* enjoyment, *your own* satisfaction.

Resources

For information on monologue workshops, contact

Karen Kohlhaas
(212) 252-4200
www.KarenKohlhaas.com

If you have found the principles of Practical Aesthetics useful in rehearsing the acting of your monologues, you may want to study them in a formal training program. Following is contact information for programs run and taught by founding Atlantic Theater Company members and authors of *A Practical Handbook for the Actor.*

The Atlantic Theater Company Acting School
453 W. 16th Street
New York, NY 10011
(212) 691-5919

American Repertory Theatre Institute for Advanced Theater Training at Harvard University
Scott Zigler, Associate Director and Head of Actor Training
(617) 495-2668
www.amrep.org

Lee Cohn
(800) 560-0093
Shuriken4@aol.com

Practical Aesthetics Australia
Melissa Bruder and Andrea Moor
P.O. Box 1543
Bondi Junction, Sydney
NSW 1355 Australia
Tel: 61 2 9358 6707
Paaustralia@ozemail.com.au

Recommended Reading

A Practical Handbook for the Actor by Melissa Bruder, Lee Cohn, Madeleine Olnek, Nathaniel Pollack, Robert Previto, and Scott Zigler. New York: Vintage Books, 1986.

True and False: Heresy and Common Sense for the Actor by David Mamet. Random House, 1997.

Make Your Voice Heard by Chuck Jones. Back Stage Books, 1996.

About the Author

Karen Kohlhaas is a founding member of the Atlantic Theater Company. She has directed plays at Atlantic and other theaters in New York and has directed and produced for radio. She is a senior teacher at the Atlantic Theater Company Acting School for New York University undergraduates and professional actors, and has taught monologue workshops since 1993.